FROM BOTH SIDES NOW

The Poetry of the Vietnam War
and Its Aftermath

Edited by
Phillip Mahony

SCRIBNER

SCRIBNER
1230 Avenue of the Americas
New York, NY 10020

Designed by Colin Joh
Set in Aldus

Manufactured in the United States of America

5 7 9 10 8 6 4

Library of Congress Cataloging-in-Publication Data

From both sides now: the poetry of the Vietnam War and its aftermath/
edited by Phillip Mahony.
p.   cm.
Poems: some translated from Vietnamese.
1. Vietnamese conflict, 1961–1975—Poetry. 2. Poetry, Modern—20th century.
I. Mahony, Phillip, date.
PN6110.V53F76   1998   98–16628
811'.54080358—dc21   CIP

ISBN 0-684-84946-1

I am surrounded by miracles.
This book is dedicated with all my love
to my wife, Marya, and our children.

Without the help of Professor Ernest Gilman of New York University, the poet and novelist Nicholas Christopher, and Glen Hartley of Writers' Representatives, Inc., this book would have never been started.

Without the help of the poet Barbara Tran, and the poet and former Marine, W. D. Ehrhart, it would have never been finished.

Thanks to them, and to all the poets.

PREFACE

For the last eighteen years, I have been fortunate enough to find employment with the New York City Police Department. A few years ago, when I was a detective in Brooklyn, I worked with another detective—let's call him Joe—who was a veteran of the Vietnam War. Like most veterans I know, Joe wasn't fond of talking about the war, but occasionally I was able to coax a story or two out of him. Once I asked Joe point blank: What it was like to be in a battle? As a cop I had been involved in a couple of shooting incidents, and both times, even though no one was hurt, and even though only three or four shots were fired in total, I was left shaken for days. In response to my question, however, Joe just shrugged. He said that basically the battles he was in, he was just shooting into the jungle, and out of the jungle someone was shooting back at him. There was a lot he wasn't telling me, of course, but that's what he said.

Then one day while we were talking, a third detective, Ted, joined us in the lunchroom. Joe informed me that Ted was a veteran as well, which was news to me. "Is that right, Ted?" I asked. Ted said nothing. Joe badgered him. "Come on, Ted, Phill here wants to hear about the war. Tell him about the war." Ted stiffened, saying something to the effect that he'd rather just eat. I tried to end it there, but Joe's badgering continued until finally Ted got up, cursed, wrapped up his food and walked away to eat somewhere else. After he was gone, Joe, seeing the confusion in my eyes, leaned toward me. "Teddy was a sniper," he explained. "He saw what he killed."

The Paris Peace Accords were signed over twenty-five years ago, but the legacy of the Vietnam War is all around us. It can be found in emotionally scarred veterans like Joe and Ted who sit quietly beside us in so many lunchrooms across the country. It can be found in the grieving families who still flock quietly to the Vietnam Veterans Memorial in Washington D.C. And nowadays it can also be found on college campuses throughout this country, where determined young students with last names like Tran and Nguyen wrestle with questions of identity and history while grabbing for their share of the American Dream.

The first thing that I want to say about this book, then, is that I put it

together in the hope that I might, as Ezra Pound instructed, "make it new."
My intention is to tell the story of the Vietnam War and its aftermath in an
updated and compelling new manner. By doing so, I hope to stimulate dis-
cussion about the war at a time when our country, although increasingly
surrounded by its aftereffects, seems all too willing to put that chapter in
our history behind us.

There is, however, a second intention to this anthology. The long
process that led to the first Xeroxing and cutting and pasting began one day
in the spring of 1995 when a small magazine assigned me to review a book
of poetry by a man named David Vancil. It was his first book, and I had
never heard of him before, but my interest was piqued because he was a
Vietnam veteran, and some of his poems were about that experience.

The assignment couldn't have come at a better time. Despite being a
lifelong lover of poetry, I had become disheartened by a sense that the
poetry world was becoming monopolized by an elitist cartel of university
creative writing teachers pumping out tediously obscure, self-referential
word games, essentially for each other. Where do these people live? I won-
dered. What insulated, enchanted streets do they walk on that they can
waste their time on such apparent meaninglessness?

Vancil's book, published by Vietnam Generation and Burning Cities
Press Inc., was different. There was a refreshing importance, a necessity to
his book that a great many collections of contemporary poetry lacked.
Reading Vancil's book started me on a mission that came to be as much
about the state of contemporary poetry as it was about the Vietnam War.
Two years of research later, that mission culminated in the compiling of
this anthology.

My second hope for this book, then, is that it might bring increased
attention and respect to poetry that is relevant, important, and readable,
poetry that aspires to *matter*, to confront and shine new light on signifi-
cant events and issues of our time.

The third thing I would like to discuss briefly is the format of this book.
The poems are arranged to simulate the progression of the Vietnam War.
The book begins with poems about the self-immolations of the Buddhist
monks in South Vietnam in the early 1960s, proceeds through the course of
the war, and ends with poems about the related unresolved issues of today.
I use the term "simulate" as opposed to "replicate" because at times strict
chronology is set aside where poems with similar themes are arranged
together for maximum effect. Most theme-oriented poetry anthologies
present their poets one after another in alphabetical or chronological order.
This anthology, however, is intended to be less a showcase for individual

poets than for the art of poetry itself, and for poetry's unique ability to explore complex issues on all their multiple levels, and in doing so to clarify, to educate, and to inform.

Finally, the title. *From Both Sides Now* refers initially of course to the Joni Mitchell song. In that song the speaker is brought to an unpleasant awareness of the sad realities of life and love. Wisdom is gained, but innocence is lost forever. The song was popular during the Vietnam War, and one can't help but look at it as a capsulation of the changes that were taking place in America during those turbulent years. As the body bags came home, Americans everywhere, like the singer in the song, were tragically awakening to things they really didn't want to know, things that would change forever their way of looking at their country, their leaders, and their place in the world.

This is a book in which opposing views come together to hopefully convey a fuller understanding of the war and its continuing impact. Included are poems by both American and Vietnamese combat veterans and by veterans of the armies of both North and South Vietnam. Also included are poems by civilians: wives and widows, children and orphans, and by protesters, those who fought as hard as they could, on both sides, to end the war.

Furthermore, the "both sides" of the conflict captured in this book is a reference to time, as this book includes not only the poetry of the past but the poetry of the present and the future. The Amerasian orphans who were abandoned by their GI fathers and Vietnamese mothers on the streets of South Vietnam and who were later, thankfully, granted citizenship into this country, are now grown and writing hard. Furthermore, the first postwar generation of Vietnamese-Americans—the children of those Vietnamese who fled to this country after the fall of Saigon, and, later, the sons and daughters of the boat people—are just now finding and exercising their unique and wonderful literary voices. Any reckoning of Vietnam War literature would be woefully incomplete without these, our new American poets.

CONTENTS

INTRODUCTION

by Stanley Karnow

I initially visited Vietnam in the summer of 1959 as *Time*'s chief Asia correspondent. Five years earlier, after the Communist-led Vietminh crushed France's attempt to restore its colonial rule, the country had been partitioned and the southern zone, now supported by the United States, seemed to be peaceful. But, on the evening of July 8, guerrillas infiltrated Bien Hoa, a South Vietnamese army base north of Saigon, killing two American military advisers, Major Dale R. Buis and Master Sergeant Chester M. Ovnand. My report of the incident earned only a few paragraphs in the magazine, and it deserved little more. For at that stage nobody could have imagined that Buis and Ovnand would head the list of nearly sixty thousand others engraved in granite on the Vietnam Memorial in Washington—or that the war that ensued was to claim the lives of at least two million Vietnamese soldiers and civilians, the majority of them slaughtered by U.S. artillery, bomber planes, and other ultramodern weapons. Looking back, it was inconceivable to me then that I had witnessed the beginning of a conflict that I would cover for the next sixteen years and analyze for decades to come. Nor could I have dreamed in those days that Vietnam would eventually enter America's culture, inspiring movies, novels, memoirs, songs, and poems of the kind that comprise this extraordinary anthology. In many ways it ranks with the Civil War as the most searing episode in the American experience.

The longest war—and first defeat in U.S. history—it had exhausted Americans. And, following the fall of Saigon in April 1975, they wanted nothing more than to forget the nightmare. They had been appalled by the televised scenes of their sons, brothers, and husbands slogging through the jungles, swamps, and rice fields of a remote land. Just as distressing were the mounting casualties that contradicted the rosy statements of officials who repeatedly promised that victory was imminent. Over the past decade, however, the public has been reexamining Vietnam. Though they graphically remember the struggle and the acrimonious debates that drove the nation to the brink of chaos, many older Americans are currently seeking to understand how and why their government became involved in Southeast Asia, and what went wrong. Members of the younger generation, who were not yet born when the war ended, have only the vaguest notions about Vietnam, yet they are eager to learn more. Veterans have also been returning to former battlefields, where often their guides are men they once fought. This trend mirrors an effort by Americans and Vietnamese to heal their wounds and, in the process, achieve a reconciliation after a tragedy that could have been avoided.

These poems, compiled by Phillip Mahony, are a welcome contribution to that reconciliation. Written by Americans and Vietnamese on both sides, some are simple, others sophisticated. Whatever their quality, they dramatize the extent to which the protagonists in the conflict shared a common ordeal. Death and devastation knew neither nationality nor ideology.

Mahony classified the poems chronologically, so that they span the length of the war. They begin in 1963 with a tribute to the Buddhist monk who immolated himself on a street in downtown Saigon to protest against the autocratic regime of Ngo Dinh Diem. I was there at the time and, like many of my colleagues, could not quite grasp the significance of what appeared to be a gruesome act. But as Trinh T. Minh-Ha puts it in her poem, the martyr was the "living torch of an entire people." Another poem on the subject by Jan Barry captures the confusion of a "boy from Tennessee" as he watches the spectacle of a Buddhist nun committing suicide.

> She sat smiling as though mocking the flames.
> Her hands, held together in prayer
> slowly parted. Suddenly, she drooped,
> sat up, then wilted in the fire. . . .
> He grinned—shivered—then softly swore:
> "Jesus! How'd we get in this crazy place?"

The thousands of U.S. combat troops who later arrived echoed that sentiment. Baffled in a strange environment in which they could not distinguish between friend and foe, they were prompted by fear to conclude that every Vietnamese was hostile. William Ehrhart, a highly decorated former Marine sergeant, caught the mood. He had enlisted, convinced that he would be applauded as a savior, as were the American forces that liberated Europe in World War II. But, as he quickly discovered, Vietnam was different.

> Nobody wears uniforms.
> They all talk
> the same language. . . .
> They tape grenades
> inside their clothes,
> and carry satchel charges
> in their market baskets . . .
> It's practically impossible
> to tell civilians
> from the Vietcong;
> after a while,
> you quit trying.

As a result, the GIs became increasingly insensitive to the carnage. Or as David Connolly, who served with the 11th Armored Cavalry Regiment, recalled:

> all kinds of bodies,
> ours, theirs, his,
> until nothin meant nothin.

Racism also poisoned numbers of Americans. Often, as they peered in disbelief at the piles of torn and twisted enemy corpses following an engagement, they had no explanation for such sacrifice except to dismiss them as "gooks" for whom the Western concept of life was alien. Reflecting the same attitude, General William Westmoreland and other U.S. officers observed, "Asians don't think about death the way we do." But the gooks they denigrated were remarkably similar to themselves—lonely, homesick, and yearning for the sweethearts they left behind. A poem by Nguyen Dinh Thi exemplifies their feelings:

> I love you, darling, as I love our land,
> suffering and wretched, yet so beautiful.

But while the horrors of Vietnam desensitized many GIs, it also aroused the conscience of some, like David Connolly, and the memory of Thach, a slain North Vietnamese corporal, was to remain with him.

> I see you still;
> your shining, black hair,
> your high cheekbones
> and bared teeth,

> your glowing, searching eyes,
> testing each step
> as if it were your last . . .
> There's no pride, no regret,
> no way I'll forget
> your death until mine.

The various other poems in this volume are equally poignant and, as a whole, they convey what to me represents the single most important message of Vietnam: Never again.

1

To Bear Any Burden

For the Memory of Thich Quang Duc
R. L. Barth

In chaos, judgment took on form and name:
The lotus flared; men burned in your just flame.

For Love of Another
Trinh T. Minh-Ha

crossed feet joined hands
a man without words without cries
    confesses his flame on the screen
behind the fire the witnesses watch
the flickering in a last tongue of flame
for a while still it burns
the living torch of an entire people
of an entire people reduced to silence
today a man burns
in a dark fire on a scarlet sky
little by little he is consumed
illuminating mute
the crowd riveted to his side
falls prostrate as the last view
is extinguished
the faithful turn over the ashes
collecting one by one the carbonized remains
out of strong desire to preserve
replace in the fire
his heart remained intact
his heart remained intact

A Nun in Ninh Hoa

Jan Barry

It was quite a sight for a boy from Tennessee:
a Buddhist nun dressed in fire
sitting proudly amid a solemn, silent crowd,
flames and a smoke plume her terrible costume.

Riding shotgun on a fuel truck convoy,
"just along for the ride,"
Jimmy Sharpe saw a sight this morning
beyond any experience he can describe.

She sat smiling as though mocking the flames.
Her hands, held together in prayer,
slowly parted. Suddenly, she drooped,
sat up, then wilted in the fire.

Safe back at the base, Jimmy's chatter
circled the nightmare he still could taste.
He grinned—shivered—then softly swore:
"Jeesus! How'd we get in this crazy place?"

When

J. Vincent Hansen

Vietnam was when
darkness covered the earth
and the oft-sighted light
at the end of the tunnel
was nothing more
than a blazing Buddhist monk.

GULF OF TONKIN
D. C. Berry

LBJ gets Congress to attack North Vietnam
because of twenty phantom torpedoes.
North Vietnam supposedly shoots them

at the US Navy, although
according to the US Navy, "Freak weather effects
and overeager sonarmen may have accounted

for many of the reports.
No actual visual sightings
by *Maddox* . . .

Turner Joy also reports no actual visual sightings
or wakes. Entire action leaves many doubts."
Nevertheless, President Johnson

gets sixteen wise men. They push
two long tables together, two oak tables
mightier than aircraft carriers. The guns

are a dozen ash trays.
It's the Year of the Dragon—time, dammit, to nail
Ho's pecker to the wall, boys, and do it today.

My fellow Amurcans, my fellow teenagers of the world,
let's rock. We can't let Uncle Ho shoot the bird
at John Wayne.

FLIGHT ORDERS
Walter McDonald

It
has come, the
pledge
of all uniforms,
the
flat spin no
jet
can rudder out
of,
suction down with
no
operative ejection seat.
War.

DEVOTION
Truong Quoc Khanh

Translated by Don Luce, John Schafer, and Jacqui Chagnon

If I were a bird
    I would be a white dove
If I were a flower
    I would be a sunflower
If I were a cloud
    I would be a warm cloud
Since I am a man
    I shall live for my country.

As a bird,
    I would fly from south to north
    Singing of Reunification.
As a flower,
    I would sow morning's Love
    In every heart that yearns for Peace.
As a cloud,
    I would float with the wind
    To freshen the heroic struggle of the past.
As a man,
    I will use every breath
    To raise the banner of independence.

What Saves Us

Bruce Weigl

We are wrapped around each other
in the back of my father's car parked
in the empty lot of the high school
of our failures, sweat on her neck
like oil. The next morning I would leave
for the war and I thought I had something
coming for that, I thought to myself
that I would not die never having
been inside her body. I lifted
her skirt above her waist like an umbrella
blown inside out by the storm. I pulled
her cotton panties up as high
as she could stand. I was on fire. Heaven
was in sight. We were drowning
on our tongues and I tried
to tear my pants off when she stopped
so suddenly we were surrounded
only by my shuddering
and by the school bells
grinding in the empty halls.
She reached to find something,
a silver crucifix on a silver chain,
the tiny savior's head
hanging, and stakes through his hands and his feet.
She put it around my neck and held me
so long my heart's black wings were calmed.
We are not always right
about what we think will save us.
I thought that dragging the angel down that night
would save me, but I carried the crucifix in my pocket
and rubbed it on my face and lips
nights the rockets roared in.
People die sometimes so near you,
you feel them struggling to cross over,
the deep untangling, of one body from another.

Doctor Able

Peter Ulisse

I often think about
words,
the way John F. Kennedy
("ask not what your country
can do for you. . . .")
glistened and gleamed
on a January podium.
I understand how syllables
can make some able
and willing
"to bear any burden, meet any
hardship."
I hear Johnson
blistering and badgering
congressmen like ants:
Gulf of Tonkin, minimum
essential force,
winning the hearts and
minds of the people.

But words fail me now
looking into my wife's eyes
simply trying to say,
"I have orders for Vietnam."

EMBARKATION
Walter McDonald

They are down, finally—
David, his legs kicked
through the ladder
miles above the floor in dreams
so far from us in our
brown parting.
Beneath him
Chuck of the dark hair
rests. How can such
bodies of chaos rest?

We hover
in the boys' nightlight,
impatient for them
to wake again.
But dreading dawn.

DEPARTURE
Xuan Moi

> *Translated by Thanh T. Nguyen and Bruce Weigl*

Looking to the top of Paradise Mountain
This night of the clear and bright moon,
Who can understand
That the more I miss our love
The stronger my love becomes.

Please be happy, my love,
Because we promised to see each other
When the clouds have disappeared.
All through the night I write this poem.
Third watch, cock-crow, everyone asleep.

Only I'm awake, writing this for you,
So exhausted I didn't know I'd fallen asleep.
My dream of you came quickly and was gone.
Vanished with the dawn's pink light.
When North and South are at peace,
We will have each other again.

Columns

Glover Davis

A column of Marine Corps trucks
stretches ahead of us into the fog.
Our headlights are frosted cones
barely touching the young marines
who lean on the tailgates and stare
out of their helmets into the past.
They blink or run their hands along
the webbing, the buckles, the straps
that would gleam in the light.
Fatigues rest like knife blades
on the shoulders and the legs
toughened with sand. I can tell
that their faces are clear as paper.
I can tell that what they expect
will never happen, and when they sleep
pushed together in the huge trucks
out on the highways of America
they remind me of the speechless
sorrows glazing the eyes of cattle.

On the Yellow Footprints

McAvoy Layne

"Well now, look at this unsightly herd,
Standin' there passin' the crud to one another
Without even movin'.
My name is Briant, girls.
I'm your mother now,
And I'm going to give you some motherly advice,
Quit on me,
And I'll show you a short cut back to the old
Neighborhood,
Right through your ass.
Is that clear!?"

"Yes, Sir!"

"I don't hear you, ladies!"

"Yes, Sir!!"

"Puberty must be hell."

"Yes, Sir!!!"

Jump School—First Day

Leroy V. Quintana

When the Sgt.,
who hadn't
said a word
about them
to anybody else,
saw that Teran
had BORN TO SUFFER
tattooed on his chest,
he made him drop,
give him twenty,
guaranteed him
he'd suffer here,
if for no other
reason.

Before Going

Lamont Steptoe

before going
to vietnam
the united states government
asked me
to bend over
spread my cheeks
and allow a white male
to insert his finger
up my asshole
only tight virgin rectums
were desired in 'nam
later
other penetrations
would occur
they said
it was to protect us against disease
but i think
they stole bits of our souls
needle by needle

Knowledge

Michael Casey

When the Command Sergeant Major
Asks ya somethin
Don't get nervous or scairt
Don't get flustrated
Say to yaself
    I'm not scairt a nothin
Stand tall an speak up proud
Ya gotta know
That ya know
What ya know
Look tall
    Whip it to me, Command Sergeant Major
    Ah know ma shit
    Whip it to me

RED HORSE

David Widup

Rapid
Equipment
Deployment

Heavy
Operational
Re-supply -
Squadron of
Engineers

Red Horse.
Formed by the same Act of Congress
as the Green Berets.
For the same purpose.
Killing people more efficiently.

We could build a bridge,
extend a runway,
repair a communication tower,
lay down an AM-2 matting chopper pad,
fix a perimeter, barbed wire and all,
put up a bomb shelter,
faster,
better,
than anyone in the world.

We were stronger,
could drink more,
sleep less,
work harder,
than anyone in the world.

Red Horse.

Red Horse training is at
Eglin Air Force Base, Florida
Field #2.
I get off the plane at 8 PM
in July
and I'm sweating so bad
I'm wet from head to toe.

The first thing I hear is
"You think this is bad,
wait till your ass is in Vietnam!"
I rethink the merits of joining the Air Force
so that they don't give me a gun
and send me to Vietnam.

For eight weeks,
I learn how to kill, maim and brutalize.
It's hotter than I can ever remember being.
At night,
I lay naked on my cot in the open bay barracks
or bed roll in the field tent
and think about stars
and my dead Mother
and sex with women
I don't even know.
I fall asleep.

Two hundred of us
sweat through Florida's hottest summer
in one hundred years
thinking that hell is hotter yet.
At the Golden Coast club,
I'm picked up by an 18 year old girl,
decades younger than me, it seems,
and wake up on the beach naked beside her
the next morning.

Red Horse.
We flew from Florida
to Alaska
to Tokyo, Japan
in a very short eternity
in the belly of a C-141.

Red Horse.
All the training
and discipline
and muscles
counted for the cube root of fuck all
when that plane nose dived
into hell.

UNTITLED

Dick Shea

so for some unknown reason
i volunteered
and am suddenly 35 thousand feet over vietnam
in a military iron bird
it was all ocean a moment ago
but now a sandy beach
and a green land
peacefully there beneath flowing white clouds
welcomes me
sarcastically
the plane bumps in
the runway is filled with holes
and armed guards
which dispel all the tranquility
gathered at 35 thousand
plane door opens
blast of hot air hits me
gangway rolls up
i exit first
cause i was designated courier of some top secret boxes
a stumbling army first lieutenant
    and a private first class approach
    chaperoned by a major
the first lieutenant impressively orders his detail
of one man
to unload the material
the private calls out the box numbers
the lieutenant shouts out a large busy impressive "check"
and puts a check behind a number
on his impressive clipboard
apparently his only function
the major stands with his hands behind his back
in a state of smiling numbness
the lieutenant importantly signs the received line
then gives me a ride to my first briefing on vietnam
i fill out numerous irritating forms
and hear only one thing at the briefing

if a suspicious looking vietnamese
brings a suspicious looking package
into a place suspiciously full of americans
and sets it down and leaves
leave with him

THE SEA AND THE SANDS
HHT

Translated by Huynh Sanh Thong

The frenzied sea is roaring day and night—
the quiet sands are cowering, lying still.
The sea's fierce hands will slap and slash the sands:
waves fly apart, sands stick together still.

The sea may flaunt and vaunt its strength, its power—
it boasts a host of sharks that maim and hurt.
The sands just smile in silence and won't budge—
the sharks will die, dirt going back to dirt.

The cruel sea, with leaping billows, tries
to wash away the sands, resistant knaves.
Puffed up with pride, the sea miscalculates;
the sands ashore yet smile and mock the waves.

The sea may slowly drain and then recede—
the sands forever will endure, intact.
Wild waves, while surging high with silver crests,
will crash and break—the sands will stay compact.

The brutal sea is only tide and surf—
with no gold sands, where could it find a bed?
O sea, remember! Deep, deep lie the sands.
When burst volcanoes, you shall bow your head!

ENTRY

David Huddle

Arrived in khakis, overseas cap, bloused boots,
I am standing with a hundred others
like me, new ones in tan at Tan Son Nhut,
crowded around some sergeant whose only words
I will remember are *Welcome to Vietnam.*
Probably he tells us to listen up,
what he has to say may save our lives. I'm
going to hear that a lot. Bad student

as usual I ignore him, gawk at faces,
the wire fence, planes landing, moving light beams.
In this heat, more plant than man, I'm breathing
slowly, registering these queer noises,
noticing all around me M-16s
slung like toys on the backs of the ones in green.

NEW GUY

Walter McDonald

I saw girls squatting against the wall,
and backed out, surely the men's shower,
and it was, the sign said it was mine,
my first day under mortars and rockets

at Tan Son Nhut. Only men lived
in those barracks. Resigned, I entered
the wide corridor of open showers.
They never glanced at me, three girls

and a wrinkled woman. This was their
stall, after so many rooms to scrub,
mops propped in buckets before them
like bamboo stakes. They seemed camped

for the day, with Asian patience.
Two other men scrubbed themselves naked
in suds, and ignored them. With miles of maps
to go over before I slept, facing the wall,

I stripped, shivered and soaped in the cold
water of Saigon, my eyes closed,
listening underwater to alien voices
like angels speaking in tongues.

GIRL AT THE CHU LAI LAUNDRY

Bruce Weigl

All this time I had forgotten.
My miserable platoon was moving out
One day in the war and I had my clothes in the laundry.
I ran the two dirt miles,
Convoy already forming behind me. I hit
The block of small hooches and saw her
Twist out the black rope of her hair in the sun.
She did not look up at me,
Not even when I called to her for my clothes.
She said I couldn't have them,
They were wet . . .

Who would've thought the world stops
Turning in the war, the tropical heat like hate
And your platoon moves out without you,
Your wet clothes piled
At the feet of the girl at the laundry,
Beautiful with her facts.

POINTMAN
(A Shau Valley, 1969)
Jon Forrest Glade

I really fucked up when I first got here.
I was with two other cherries
and the Lieutenant asked where we were from.
They were from Chicago and L.A.
When I said I was from Wyoming,
the Lieutenant just smiled and said
had I ever been hunting before?
I told him my father had been an outfitter,
a professional hunting guide.
He put his hands on my shoulder and said,
"Congratulations, you're my new pointman."
I asked him for Christ's sakes why?
He asked if I knew which way was north,
so I turned and pointed true north.
He said, "That's why."

I should have told him I was from
some big, smoggy city, and had never seen
the sun or the sky or the stars before.

POEM OF HOPE

Thien Ly

Translated by Don Luce, John Schafer, and Jacqui Chagnon

Those of you who die for tomorrow
Those who still live for the future,
Don't you feel the hopes of today
Rise up as the flag flies in the wind?
Don't you hear your heart beat loudly,
The voice of hope mingled with the joyful songs of victory?
Some days ago we could not sleep
Waiting for people to come to break the yoke of oppression,
Anxiously waiting the day!
People
Rise up like the forest and mountains!

The blood of the people flows strongly
Don't hesitate! Stand up and fly the large flag!
The road of freedom resounds with cheering voices.
How great is the violence of the enemy but our forces can
    resist.
Stand in a multitude of lines and go forward
Trampling and smashing the herd of white-faced enemies.

Even though the bullets kill by mistake,
The Mother still calmly rocks the baby
And the baby grows up unafraid of the bombing.
Cut into pieces the bodies of those who sell our country!
Don't withdraw no matter how strong the enemy!
Remember to prepare the meal for those who sit up late to
    watch the enemy.
In the distance we joyfully see thousands of stars,
And imagine that these are our flags fluttering in the sky.

Today
Our whole nation begins to rise up,
Prepare yourself! Young men and women now suffering
    many difficulties.
Let us join together to enter a glorious period,
Raise the flag of victory!

Over one century of struggle
But now, today
Thousands of eyes shine with hope.

FIRST ENCOUNTER

Leroy V. Quintana

You have stopped for a break, stand up
to put your gear on and hear shots,
see the flash of the muzzles.
You have been followed.
The whiteness of the branches
that have been cut along the way
tells you you're on a new trail,
but the sergeant is a stateside G.I.:
barracks inspections, rules and regs.
You are probably surrounded.
There are five others beside you.
You are twenty-three.
You look quickly around you:
the sky, the trees.
You're far from home.
You know now that your life
is no longer yours.

Corporal Thach
First Confirmed NVA Kill

David Connolly

I see you still;
your shining, black hair,
your high cheekbones
and bared teeth,
your glowing, searching eyes,
testing each step
as if it were your last.

You flinched
as the angry hornets
I let fly
snapped you up
then let you drop,
a jumble of arms and legs
and black and white scarf.

Your last reflex
killed the man next to me
but it's your death
I remember.

There's no pride, no regret,
no way I'll forget
your death until mine.

THE FIRST

Leroy V. Quintana

Booker said the first time
he saw somebody killed
a gook came charging,
probably high on grass.
Garcia, the machine gunner, opened up,
and the gook just seemed to hang
in the air as the rounds ripped
through him for what seemed minutes.

Oh, how he had been wronged
by being sent to the Nam.
Booker, who kept live rounds in his weapon
during inspection, hoping for a discharge,
who was so dreadfully fainthearted under fire.

FIRST ONE

Jim Nye

Roll him over carefully
Align his body
    on an axis, east to west
Fold his hands across his chest
    close his eyes

He is gone
But we remember
    and talk softly
Someone gathers his gear
Another wipes his face

We cannot explain
This
Avoiding each other's eyes
No one told us
We did not know.

    To come to this
    After so long a short life
    A child surrounded by children
    Playing—

First Casualty

Kevin Bowen

They carried him slowly
down the hill.
One hand hung,
gray and freckled.
No one spoke but
stared straight up.
His body, heavy,
rolled back and forth
on the litter.
At LZ Sharon cooks spooned
the last hot food.
One by one the squad
walked back uphill.
"Don't mean nothing,"
someone said.
But all that winter
and into spring
I swear he followed us,
his soul, a surplice
trailing the jungle floor.

It Don't Mean Nothin

David Connolly

On his second day there,
they went down into Bien Hoa city
with their brand new guns,
just hours after the VC had left,
and strolled along a wide,
European style boulevard
lined with blossoming trees
and the bloating bodies
of Americans, dead for days.

He puzzled at their leader,
the nineteen year old veteran
with the pale, yellow skin,
bleached, rotting fatigues,
and crazy, crazy eyes,
who hawked brown phlegm
on each dead American saying,
"That don't mean nothin;
y'hear me, meat?"

And everywhere he went,
there were more,
down all the days and nights,
all kinds of bodies,
ours, theirs, his,
until nothin meant nothin.

2

Just a Touch on the Trigger

Of Late

George Starbuck

"Stephen Smith, University of Iowa sophomore, burned what
    he said was his draft card"
and Norman Morrison, Quaker, of Baltimore Maryland,
    burned what he said was himself.
You, Robert McNamara, burned what you said was a concen-
    tration of the Enemy Aggressor.
No news medium troubled to put it in quotes.

And Norman Morrison, Quaker, of Baltimore Maryland,
    burned what he said was himself.
He said it with simple materials such as would be found in
    your kitchen.
In your office you were informed.
Reporters got cracking frantically on the mental disturbance
    angle.
So far nothing turns up.

Norman Morrison, Quaker, of Baltimore Maryland, burned,
    and while burning, screamed.
No tip-off. No release.
Nothing to quote, to manage to put in quotes.
Pity the unaccustomed hesitance of the newspaper editorialists.
Pity the press photographers, not called.

Norman Morrison, Quaker, of Baltimore Maryland, burned
    and was burned and said
all that there is to say in that language.
Twice what is said in yours.
It is a strange sect, Mr. McNamara, under advice to try
the whole of a thought in silence, and to oneself.

NORMAN MORRISON*

David Ferguson

Not an unhappy man
but one who could not stand
in the silence of his mind
the cathedral
emptied of its ritual
and sounding about his ears
like a whirlwind.

He cradled the child awhile
then set her down nearby
and spoke in a tongue of flame
near the Pentagon
where they had no doubt.

> Other people's pain
> can turn so easily
> into a kind of play.
> There's beauty
> in the accurate
> trajectory. Death
> conscripts the mind
> with its mysterious
> precision.

*Suicide by self-immolation in front of the Pentagon, November 2, 1965.

I Kneel Down and Pray

Nhat Chi Mai

Translated by Don Luce, John Schafer, and Jacqui Chagnon

Why do Americans burn themselves?*
Why do non-Vietnamese demonstrate all over the world?
Why does Viet Nam remain silent
And not dare to utter the word Peace?

I feel helpless
And I suffer
If alive I cannot express myself.
I will offer my life to show my aspirations.

Is appealing for Peace a crime?
Is acting for Peace communism?
I am appealing for Peace
In the name of Man

I join my hands and kneel down;
I accept this utmost pain in my body
In hope that the words of my heart be heard.
Please stop it, my fellowmen!

Please stop it, my fellowmen!
More than twenty years have elapsed.
More than twenty years of bloodshed;
Do not exterminate my people!
Do not exterminate my people!

I join my hands and kneel down to pray.

Signed: Nhat Chi Mai
The one who burns herself for peace.

*Norman Morrison, the American pacifist who burned himself in front of
the Pentagon on November 2, 1965, is highly regarded in South Vietnam
and a hero in the North.

THE INSERT

R. L. Barth

Our view of sky, jungle, and fields constricts
Into a sink hole covered with saw-grass

Undulating, soon whipped slant as the chopper
Hovers at four feet. Rapt, boot deep in slime,

We deploy ourselves in loose perimeter,
Listening for incoming rockets above

The thump of rotor blades; edgy for contact,
Junkies of terror impatient to shoot up.

Nothing moves, nothing sounds; then, single file,
We move across a streambed toward high ground.

The terror of the insert's quickly over.
Too quickly . . . And more quickly every time . . .

TAKING AIM

Walter McDonald

Stalking through jungles
this is the way
you hold your M-16,

muzzle down,
sniffing
like a hundred-dollar dog.

Keep it on automatic.
Anything moves in the bushes
you open fire:

this damn '16
will rise for you
and point the bastard out.

Kind of pull it sideways,
like this.
Don't aim the damn thing:

point it.
And don't forget: just a touch
on the trigger.

If you're holding it
like this
it'll get him.

The Next Step

W. D. Ehrhart

The next step you take
may lead you into an ambush.

The next step you take
may trigger a tripwire.

The next step you take
may detonate a mine.

The next step you take
may tear your leg off at the hip.

The next step you take
may split your belly open.

The next step you take
may send a sniper's bullet through your brain.

The next step you take.
The next step you take.

The next step.
The next step.

The next step.

Humpin' Through the Boonies

Dale Ritterbusch

Get down—a sniper's rd ricochets to the right,
where? anyone got it? off to the left, the
tree line, eleven o'clock, no, to the front,
rake the tree line, nothing, let's go,
spread out, keep your distance—
more harassment than anything, getting
down in the dirt, sucking dust all afternoon—
another rd, another hundred yards, heavy pack,
hot helmet, sweat pouring into the eyes,
and they watch, unaffected by everything,
dry dirt caking the sweat—fuck the army,
FTA on the helmet ahead of me, check out
the hedgerow—so thick a bangalore
wouldn't make a dent—stay away from the gate,
wring out the sweat, watch for tripwires, a spider's
thread in the sun, canteen half full, warm, not
worth the effort—another rd, 2, 3, AK by the sound
keep moving, keep awake up there, hold it, hold it!,
movement, sleight of hand, what's up? get to the
hamlet late afternoon, don't take no shit, not today,
too many days (exactly) like this, hey! pump a 79 rd
over there 150 m, edge of the dike, to the right
20 m—another rd zings in, the flash, the explosion—
wait, get up, nothing, they're gone, nobody's there
except old women, kids, a few dogs
fuck this shit, zippo diplomacy, they were here dammit
can smell it, all that rice for the women, bullshit,
nothing, again nothing, check that hootch
do it right this time, ain't no damn social call,
no shit?, burn it, two klicks and we're there,
not the easy way, dumbshit, through the paddy—
call it in, ETA LZ Red, 17:15, move it out,
hear them damn birds, let's go, second squad
mount up, the rotor wash cool, too tired
even to sweat, anyway.

No Slack

Jim Nye

Sitting on a sandbag
Drinking a warm beer.
I watched him sitting cross-legged.
19 years old, should've been
At a high school game
Hitting on a cheerleader
Grinning and talking
Instead, slowly, methodically
Slipping rounds into a magazine
Placing each filled magazine in its stack.
Four stacks of 5 each.
6 grenades all in a row.
6 days, rations to be packed.
Rubber tubing tied on each ankle
For tourniquets, just in case.
Four canteens laced with iodine tablets.
A helmet with No Slack carefully penciled across it.
Writing paper and pencil wrapped in plastic.
He looked up and saw me watching—

Airborne, sir
Roger that, I said . . .
Roger, that.

A Young Man's Recollection

Ky Niem Thanh Dang

Translated by Thanh T. Nguyen and Bruce Weigl

On the battlefield at sunset I met Thanh,
Our guns on our shoulders, our skin brown from sun.
That moment of exile, we sang a song
Of our people's love spread across the front.

Like regret that moment of separation stays in our hearts.
The moon had nothing to show but its closed eyes.
Standing shoulder to shoulder, there were no words,
And now only this poem to remember our friendship.

No Lie, GI

David Connolly

We had a deal, he and I,
of no bullshit between us.
If one of us got wounded,
the other wouldn't lie.
So when he got hit
and he asked me,
"How's my leg?"
I looked him straight in the eye
and told him, "It's fine."
It looked fine to me,
laying over there,
looked as good as new.

GUERRILLA WAR
W. D. Ehrhart

It's practically impossible
to tell civilians
from the Vietcong.

Nobody wears uniforms.
They all talk
the same language.
(and you couldn't understand them
even if they didn't).

They tape grenades
inside their clothes,
and carry satchel charges
in their market baskets.

Even their women fight;
and young boys.
and girls.

It's practically impossible
to tell civilians
from the Vietcong;

after a while,
you quit trying.

Luck

Pauline Hebert

The red cross wasn't bulletproof,
        The hospital
Fair game. Incoming rounds knew no mercy.
        If you had a stethoscope
In your ears when the first mortar landed
        You, your patients
Could wind up dead, all of them,
        Your responsibility
To save, to keep safe.
        There was never time
To save them all,
        There was never time
To take cover,
        There was never time
To listen
        There was never Silence.

Above the tunnels of Cu Chi,
        In Quonset huts,
We perched stationary,
        Sitting ducks
Without sandbags, bunkers,
        The only thing
Between us and forever,
        Luck,
Geneva conventions be damned.

CONDEMNATION

Thich Nhat Hanh

Listen to this:
yesterday six Vietcong came through my village,
and because of this, the village was bombed.
Every soul was killed.
When I returned to the village the next day,
there was nothing but clouds of dust—
the pagoda without roof or altar,
only the foundations of houses,
the bamboo thickets burned away.

Here in the presence of the undisturbed stars,
in the invisible presence of all people still alive on Earth,
let me raise my voice to denounce this dreadful war,
this murder of brothers by brothers!

Whoever is listening, be my witness:
I cannot accept this war.
I never could, I never will.
I must say this a thousand times before I am killed.

I am like the bird who dies for the sake of its mate,
dripping blood from its broken beak and crying out,
"Beware! Turn around and face your real enemies—
ambition, violence, hatred, and greed."

Humans are not our enemies—even those called "Vietcong."
If we kill our brothers and sisters, what will we have left?
With whom then shall we live?

SCHOOLDAY IN MAN QUANG*

Denis Knight

On Thursday a Vietcong flag was noticed flying
Above the village of Man Quang in South Vietnam.
Therefore Skyraider fighter-bombers were sent in,
Destroying the village school and other "structures."
The bombing mission killed an estimated 34 schoolchildren,
And three adults.

From Man Quang survivors of the raid, not pacified,
Tried to carry the coffins into Da Nang as a protest;
But were held in security by Government forces,
Who made an indemnification over the children's bodies;
And arrested the parents.

There is no information about lessons in progress
When the school died: perhaps civics, a foreign language,
Or the catechism; or "Practical Subjects"—pottery,
Domestic science, woodwork, metalwork: in darkness
Burning, dying.

On Thursday a Vietcong flag was noticed flying.

*This incident was reported from Saigon on March 18 and March 25,
1965, by the special correspondent of the London *Times.*

IMAGINARY UNIVERSES
Allen Ginsberg

Under orders to shoot the spy, I discharged
    my pistol into his mouth.
He fell face down from the position life
    left his body kneeling blindfold.

No, I never did that. Imagined in airport snow,
    Albany plane discharging passengers.

Yes, the Mexican-faced boy, 19
    in Marine cloth, seat next me
Descending Salt Lake, accompanied his
    brother's body from Vietnam.
"The Gook was kneeling in front of me,
    crying & pleading. There were two;
    he had a card we dropped on them."
The card granted immunity to those
    V.C. surrendering.
"On account of my best friend &
    my brother I killed both Gooks."
That was true, yes.

    February 1969

We Never Know

Yusef Komunyakaa

He danced with tall grass
for a moment, like he was swaying
with a woman. Our gun barrels
glowed white-hot.
When I got to him,
a blue halo
of flies had already claimed him.
I pulled the crumbled photograph
from his fingers.
There's no other way
to say this: I fell in love.
The morning cleared again,
except for a distant mortar
& somewhere choppers taking off.
I slid the wallet into his pocket
& turned him over, so he wouldn't be
kissing the ground.

Blood Trail

Jon Forrest Glade

I had a man in my sights
and I pulled the trigger.
I knew he would fall,
but I didn't think
he would get back up
and run like a wounded deer.

We followed the blood trail
and found only an abandoned pack.
The Lieutenant took the cash,
the men divided the food,
Intelligence was sent the love letters
and I got the credit
for a probable kill.
Intelligence reported the letters
were from a woman in the southern provinces.
Which meant she was arrested,
beaten, raped, locked in a tiger cage,
forced to eat her own excrement
and beaten again.

If she confessed, she was executed.
If she refused to confess, she was executed.
It was a funny war.
I shot a man.
I killed a woman.

INTELLIGENCE

Dale Ritterbusch

The body was lying there in the open,
stretched out along hedgerow
intersecting a dike—
unusual since they went to great lengths
to remove all their dead.

I thought it a trick—an easy ambush
as the platoon was bunched up
waiting for the body to be searched—
I had everyone spread out, take cover,
and search the wood line that formed
a broad L to our front.

But we weren't really that close for an
effective ambush—unless the area
was targeted by mortars,
so I thought it booby-trapped and told
everyone to back off, to get behind the dike—

I had two guys put a noose around
the neck of the corpse and fall back.
I told everyone to get down and then
gave the order to pull—

Both men were squatting behind the dike
and they yanked—hard—and fell back,
tumbling over each other as the head pulled off
and everyone laughed—the rest of the body barely moved
it had been laying there too long—

Even my old experienced E-6,
who never cracked a smile, laughed
at the two yahoos grinning, falling over each other.
"Shit for brains, you two could fuck up a wet dream,"
and we laughed; the head rolled and looked up at the sky.

We emptied a magazine into the corpse;
I thought that would set off any
pressure-release type device,

and then it was searched—nothing—
no orders, no maps, nothing—not even
a picture of his wife or his kids.

Untitled

Gerald McCarthy

We found him
his chest torn open,
shirt sticky brown.
A corporal with a bayonet
cut off his ears,
and kicked the body
in passing.

Yearning

Nguyen Dinh Thi

Translated by Huynh Sanh Thong

Whom do the stars yearn for? They blink and gleam,
lighting the path of soldiers through the clouds.
Cold night: whom does the fire yearn for? It glows
and warms the soldiers' hearts beneath dense trees.

I love you, darling, as I love our land,
suffering and wretched, yet so beautiful.
I miss you so, at each step of my way,
at mealtime every day, each night in bed.

The stars that light the dark will never dim:
loving each other, we'll struggle till we win.
The campfire in the forest flares bright red:
loving each other, proudly we'll live life.

War Story
Gerald McCarthy

Med Building

They brought the dead
in helicopters and trucks
and tried to piece the bodies back together,
shoved them in plastic bags
to be sent home.
Sometimes there was an arm or leg
leftover,
it lay around until the next shipment;
they made it fit in somewhere.

Counting Small-Boned Bodies
Robert Bly

Let's count the bodies over again.

If we could only make the bodies smaller,
The size of skulls,
We could make a whole plain white with skulls in the
        moonlight!

If we could only make the bodies smaller,
Maybe we could get
A whole year's kill in front of us on a desk!

If we could only make the bodies smaller,
We could fit
A body into a finger-ring, for a keepsake forever.

My Blood, My Bones
Nguyen Ngoc Phuong

> *Translated by Don Luce, John Schafer, and Jacqui Chagnon*

My blood flows
To cleanse the subservient spirit
My bones will be piled like a staircase
So younger brothers and sisters can walk up
        to the tower of Freedom.

THE WOMAN HE KILLED

Elliot Richman

I was doorgunner in a Huey,
flak-jacketed,
visor down,
when a VC lady leaped from high grass
in a hot LZ
amid swirling dust
and bellowing rotor blades.

Lurching off the earth
in the frenzied buck of the chopper
we stared face to face.

Black hair waving in Laotian wind,
blouse rustling in updraft
she looked so young and beautiful
even as she attempted to blow me
away with a handgun,
the only weapon she had.

And I who didn't want to bust
even one cap in her heart
fired my weapon on Rock & Roll.

So the dance we did
was under tracer light
with mad machine-gun music,
her black blouse unbuttoning,
torso sawing in half
as if caressed by a chain saw
before sinking
into sheets of dust.

Where Does It End?

Jeff Miller

The strife and fighting continue into the night.
The mechanical birds sound of death
As they buzz overhead spitting fire
Into the doomed towns where women and children
Run and hide in the bushes and ask why,
Why are we not left to live our own lives?

In the pastures, converted into battlefields,
The small metal pellets speed through the air,
Pausing occasionally to claim another victim.
A teenager from a small Ohio farm
Clutches his side in pain, and,
As he feels his life ebbing away,
He, too, asks why,
Why is he dying here, thousands of miles from home,
Giving his life for those who did not even ask for his help.

The War Without a Purpose marches on relentlessly,
Not stopping to mourn for its dead,
Content to wait for its end,
But all that the frightened parents who still have
        their sons hear is:
"the end is not in sight."

February 14, 1966

*Jeffrey Miller was one of the students killed by the National Guard at Kent State University, May 4, 1970.

Night Crossing

Giang Nam

Translated by Don Luce, John Schafer, and Jacqui Chagnon

The boat was coming in the dead of night,
Clusters of bamboo, rising tide.
The oars shook the starry sky,
A stray bird circled above,
Noiselessly the boat came in the dark,
As searchlights swept the tops of the palms.
Guns loaded, eyes wide open,
We waited.

The sampan girl had rolled up the legs of her trousers,
A cold wind blew in from the shore,
As she helped load our packs on board,
Bringing the scent of flowers and dry grass
From the forests and mountains.
As our hands touched we imagined her cheeks blushed red,
I felt her warm breath, sensed her quick gestures.

Heavily laden, the boat pulled.
"May we help you, Comrade?" I asked.
She shook her head and made the sampan turn fast.
Living in the midst of enemy posts and blockhouses,
She was used to containing joy and sorrow.

The boat went out into the darkness,
As the tide kept rising.
The oars again shook heaven and stars,
On the other bank, the palms beckoned us.
The sampan girl kept her eyes fixed
On the distant watchtower at the village entrance.
Her nimble hands worked the oars,
Her slender silhouette loomed over the river.
A few more strokes! The bank was now close,
Tender joy welled up in our hearts.
A burst of gunfire tore the night,
Sparks flew in the darkness.
"Sit still," she said, "don't move!"
The boat kept advancing towards the enemy.

It gave a lurch, bullets whizzed overhead,
Her silhouette towered over the waves.
"Sit down, sister, we will row," we pleaded.
"No, brothers, don't worry." Again the boat moved forward.

The whole dark sky was in turmoil,
Our hearts ached, our eyes shone with anger
Enemy slugs swept the river,
In our hands, our rifles burned with hatred.

The boat was now safely moored to a tree,
We were forced to leave quickly,
But slowly shook the girl's hand,
"Thank you," we whispered.
A smile lighted her face as she shook her head,
"I'm a member of the Revolutionary Youth," she said,
"I've only done my duty."
Her figure faded in the night.
As we marched across the village,
We still heard her muffled steps.

Valiant girl, your memory
Is alive in our hearts
As we press on to other battles.

GIFTS AS TOKENS OF LOVE

Tran Da Tu

Translated by Huynh Sanh Thong

To you I'll give a coil of wire, barbed wire,
the climbing vine of all this modern age—
it's coiling tight around our soul today.
Take it as my love token—don't ask why.

To you I'll give a car of plastic bombs
that will explode amidst some crowded street—
they will explode and shatter flesh to shreds.
This is the way we live—you understand?

To you I'll give the war that's killing now,
killing our homeland, many mothers' land,
where people dine on bullets and on bombs,
where cloth runs short for children's mourning bands.

To you I'll give the gift of twenty years
or seven thousand nights of cannon fire.
For seven thousand nights it's sung to you—
have you dozed off or are you still awake?

I want to give you many other things.
Enough—take just one more: a tear gas bomb.
With neither grief nor joy, my own tear glands
are gushing as I just sit here and wait.

CAVES

Michael S. Harper

Four M-48 tank platoons ambushed
near Dak To, two destroyed:
the Ho Chi Minh Trail boils,
half my platoon rockets
into stars near Cambodia,
foot soldiers dance from highland woods
taxing our burning half:

there were no caves for them to hide.

We saw no action,
eleven months twenty-two days
in our old tank
burning sixty feet away:
I watch them burn inside out:
hoisting through heavy crossfire,
hoisting over turret hatches,
hoisting my last burning man
alive to the ground,
our tank artillery shells explode
killing all inside:
hoisting blown burned squad
in tank's bladder,
plug leaks with cave blood:

there were no caves for them to hide—

TUNNELS

Yusef Komunyakaa

Crawling down headfirst into the hole,
he kicks the air & disappears.
I feel like I'm down there
with him, moving ahead, pushed
by a river of darkness, feeling
blessed for each inch of the unknown.
Our tunnel rat is the smallest man
in the platoon, in an echo chamber
that makes his ears bleed
when he pulls the trigger.
He moves as if trying to outdo
blind fish easing toward imagined blue,
pulled by something greater than life's
ambitions. He can't think about
spiders & scorpions mending the air,
or care about bats upside down
like gods in the mole's blackness.
The damp smell goes deeper
than the stench of honey buckets.
A web of booby traps waits, ready
to spring into broken stars.
Forced onward by some need,
some urge, he knows the pulse
of mysteries & diversions
like thoughts trapped in the ground.
He questions each root.
Every cornered shadow has a life
to bargain with. Like an angel
pushed up against what hurts,
his globe-shaped helmet
follows the gold ring his flashlight
casts into the void. Through silver
lice, shit, maggots, & vapor of pestilence,
he goes, the good soldier,
on hands & knees, tunneling past
death sacked into a blind corner,
loving the weight of the shotgun
that will someday dig his grave.

THE LABYRINTH

Elliot Richman

Bent double like a palsied humpbacked worm,
I slithered through the tunnels under Nam,
no longer human in form, a killer of men,
a dark rabbit in Alice's white hole,
a mad hatter in Richard Nixon's holy war.
Armed only with a silenced pistol
and a K-Bar dipped in dink's blood
I crawled through shit that smelled like fish
or the crotch of a two-bit Tu Do whore.
Half blind from tear gas, half mad from malice,
squashing under my fingers giant jungle ants
or strangling snakes with the strength of men,
I sought what lurked in the darkness below,
knowing already the horror above. Once,
I found a gook's lair stinking of death
and napalm wounds, gangrene like mustard gas
or hag's breath. One had been dead for days.
After I shot the other two, I sensed her silence
in the darkness and turned my light, catching
her maddened face in the gloom, her legs
spread apart as the child slipped from her
without even a wail, knowing already the ways
of this war. I wanted to help. I reached out
to cut the cord when she lunged at me
with a stick grenade, the baby tied to her.
I slit her throat. The child was still born.
Westmoreland talks now about "The light
at the end of the tunnel." And I ask you,
"What does that asshole know of tunnels?"

SEARCH AND DESTROY

Dale Ritterbusch

They came out of the hootch
with their hands up—surrendered—
and we found all that rice
and a couple of weapons. They
were tagged and it all seemed so easy—
too easy, and someone started to torch
the hootch and I stopped him—something
was funny. We checked the hootch
a couple times more; I had them probe it
like we were searching for mines and
a lucky poke with a knife
got us the entrance to a tunnel.
We didn't wait for any damn
tunnel clearers—we threw down
CS and smoke and maybe two hundred
yards to our right two gooks popped up
and we got 'em running across the field,
nailed 'em before they hit the trees.
We went to the other hole and popped more
gas arid smoke and a fragmentation grenade
and three gooks came out coughing, tears
and red smoke pouring out of their eyes and
nose. We thought there were more
so we threw in another grenade and one of the
dinks brought down his arms, maybe he started
to sneeze with all that crap running out of his face,
maybe he had a weapon concealed, I didn't know,
so I greased him. Wasn't much else I could do.
A sudden move like that.

Let Us Stand Up

Thai Nguyen

Translated by Don Luce, John Schafer, and Jacqui Chagnon

Let us stand up, young people,
Let the blood in our hearts rise like the tide,
Our steps sound like a storm in the night,
Our voices reach from the earth to the heavens.
Look, for haven't you seen
That it's time we break from our prison
End our years of misery;
Our food is still watered with sweat
As we remember our years in slavery,
Let us call to one another,
My suffering friends,
The road opens in front of our eyes,
The road is open and waits for our steps
To the festival of Independence.
Twenty-five years without raising our voices,
Twenty-five years of waiting;
The fire of hatred burns in our hearts
And our hands are dry and burnt,
Yet bamboo spears shall break the steel blades;
Each step, a new hope
Each song, a new glory.
Friends from North to South,
We are together, we are one,
The storm will be over,
The day of homecoming is near!
Fire will light our road,
Flags will fly on our way,
We will meet at the glorious day,
Lac Hong* blood will make our land greener,
Rice and milk will become plenty.
Hear the proud lullaby of our white-haired mother:
"The day you left, you were fifteen;
Now your feet are covered with scars
And your dreams have become bright."

Let us rise while the blaze brightens our land,
Let us rise, my brothers and sisters,
Fulfill our dream—our glorious country
Our flag of independence!

> *Lac Hong: In Vietnamese mythology, Lac Hong is the eldest son of Lac
> Long (Dragon Lord) and a fairy named Au Co. He was the founder of the
> first dynasty recognized in legend as truly Vietnamese. Thus, Lac Hong
> blood is the blood of those who are truly Vietnamese.

VIPER

(A Shau Valley, 1969)

Jon Forrest Glade

Once, when we were in the jungle,
I remember watching three GIs
trying to kill a snake.
They were armed with machetes
and entrenching tools
and were chasing it back and forth.
Maybe if they had left it alone,
it would have just gone away;
but they were trying to kill it
because it was probably a viper.

Vipers were known as Grass Snakes
and Leaf Snakes and Bamboo Snakes,
but more commonly as
Two Step Snakes.
If one bit you
you could take two steps
before you died.
It would have been simpler
and a lot safer to shoot it,
but the noise would have given
our position away;
and Charlie was deadlier
than any snake.

The viper was fast and agile
and the grunts
were too frightened to get
within more than a few feet.
I thought the whole thing was funny
until they chased it my way.

BANDED KRAITS

Kevin Bowen

Blackburn saw him first,
called us over
just as he poked his head up,
four of us
hovering over the hole
at the bottom of the slumped pile
of sandbags
at the old French base camp.
He lingered a second,
then quick as it took
to take our measure,
squirmed back down,
flipping his tail at us
as if in some obscene gesture.
But already the gasoline
was on its way. Morales
held the five-gallon can
carefully over the hole
as we watched to see
if the snake would crawl out again
as gas sifted into dirt
and the thin slit in the earth
that was his home
disappeared and reappeared
in slow migrations of sand
that seemed the pulse
of somebody's heart
we couldn't remember

until Morales dropped a match
and the blaze slunk down
the hole after.

He came out slowly.
One good shot
straight through the head
put him away.
We laid him out,
all four feet of him and fangs.
Enough time to smoke a cigarette
was what he'd give you.
The same that we gave him.
Then, babies, someone said.
We smoked and joked
our way to the green line.
Cambodia, the rains, June's weeping light.

THE HOMESICK PATROL
II Corps, Republic of Vietnam, 1969

David Vancil

One of my fingers hooked into the belt
loop of the guy leading me to a place
on the green map—six numbers that marked our
spot. While fat mosquitoes waltzed in my sweat,
a bitch-moon watched me move with an evil
eye. Behind me my sergeant counted on
me to get him home, clinging close. He glued
his ear to the hissing black radio
and stuck his mouth to the mouthpiece, ready
to report. I was the lieutenant. So
I practiced coordinates, while like a blind
man, I followed our unfamiliar host
down a well-worn trail, praying for quiet
and to walk complete through the starry night.

Ambush

Doug Anderson

In the village we unsling our rifles,
drop our packs, light cigarettes, eat, piss,
sleep fly-covered in the heat.
A round comes by my ear, an angry wasp,
and crabwise I scuttle for a hole that isn't there.
There is shouting everywhere, someone is hit.
I see the lieutenant point his pistol with both hands;
a water buffalo is bearing down on him,
stampeded by the shooting. Beside a cistern,
a monk, saffron robed, squats and laughs.
There is a woman running past
tripping on her ao dai, but no, it's not.
Before I can shout a warning the garment comes unsashed,
instead of womanflesh, an automatic rifle
flashes in an arc, and firing from the hip,
the man runs for his life.
Someone trying to duck smashes my nose with his elbow.
It is now quiet. Seven bodies lie in the village road;
three are ours, more are wounded.
My cigarette not gone halfway I begin to treat them.

Near Laos

Bill Jones

1

just outside the wire
A Recon patrol walks
Almost jauntily
Into an L-shaped ambush
Automatic weapons pop
And in between staccato bursts
High pitched voices
Scream for salvation.
"Come on," Hutch says,
"We got to help them."

As we rush blind
To join the fire-fight
Slaughter
I realize
They are dying down there
Stop
And cleverly fumble with gear
Grasp for excuses
To let Hutch go
Alone.
There are dim truths
About ourselves
We are far better
Not knowing.

Easily So easily
I could have lived
With a glance of scowling
Revulsion
Grown old and comfortable
In the shadow of cowardice.
Borne forty years of guilt.
Almost anything . . . really.
("Come on," Hutch says.)
Except the look of fleeting
Haunting
Surprise.

2

We help a Corpsman drag
A trembling Black kid
Gut-shot and eyes rolling white
Through red dust
And smoldering tree stumps

He calls alternately for Mamma
Jesus
And a buddy named Rock.
Finding no help there
He stuffs my shirtsleeve
In his mouth
And chews away the pain.

AMBUSH

Lamont Steptoe

The vibes were wrong
So he
warned his friend/survivor
As he
turned and tried
to run
out the open end
of the horse-shoe ambush
A fifty-one caliber machine gun
cut him in half
like a hoagie
he would never
see again
The last thing
he told his legs was to run
they kept running
leaving the half with
the brains and heart
dead on the ground

I STAND HERE

Lieutenant Nguyen van Nghia

Translated by Rick Murphy and Nguyen Dinh Thich

I guard my post this evening
At the end of Ben Hai Bridge.
The steady blue current below
Is like a blood vein joining North to South.
Green rice fields reflect in my badge.
Our nation's flag was handed down to us
       by our loving mother.
Each passing moment reminds me that
My parents and native land
Have entrusted this son with the nation's fate.

Standing before the gusts of wind
And the enemy's front line,
Son, never forget.
Though seven years have passed
Remember all my advice:
Man your post proudly each evening
For the glory of the motherland.
Though the wind may howl and the rain pour
Keep looking forward.
Word has come over the loudspeaker;
We are to head South.
My beloved home village fades in the distance.

I miss the harvest season
I miss the girls of home
Hair longer than one's outstretched arm.
Now the girls valiantly defend our village.
Hue knows peace and tranquility;
The Perfume River sings.
My native village knows hunger.
Every night the echoes of Southern gunfire
Tear at my insides.

Lament of Ben Hai River

"Ben Hai River" or "Hien Luong River" meaning
"kind and honest," is situated at the 17th Parallel,
the temporary demarcation line between the
Northern zone and the Southern zone of Vietnam

Nhat Hanh

Translated by the author and Helen Coutant

From here to there, hardly a hundred yards
But who has barred the bridge?
On both sides,
   the hearts wither and feel sore.
The more we hate the enemy,
   the more we love each other.

In the sky, birds swiftly glide,
In the water, fish freely swim.
Why does this road stop here?
We must tread them down, and march on.

Only a river to cross, yet how far it is!
Who severs South from North,
   wives from husbands?
We both bathe in the same water,
But it is clear on one side,
   muddy on the other.

How our hearts ache!
Streams may dry up,
   and mountains fall
But your heart will never change.
We have a debt of love, eternal love.
The enemy may split this river into
   two currents,
Into the sea they flow and merge.

HOME

Te Hanh

Translated by Nguyen Ngoc Bich

Seven years we've been away,
and my son just turned four.
They ask him: Are you from Hanoi?
He snaps back: No, I'm from the South!

He's never seen the South, but his young heart
still loves, desires, expects to return.
How can the enemy succeed in slitting off
the arteries where, for a thousand years,
blood has flowed freely?

FROM MY HEART OF HEARTS

Lieutenant Nguyen van Nghia

Translated by Rick Murphy and Nguyen Dinh Thich

The enemy guns thunder
More madly with each passing moment,
Marking the fall of many of my friends;
They will never know life again.
The motherland weeps for them.
How can we possibly surrender?
We are the proud soldiers of the bridge,
Bearers of the Party's teachings.
We must silence the enemy,
Still them like glassy waters.

I stand here, defending factories and farms.
Day and night they bustle with activity
So the motherland will be blessed in wartime.
I stand here so my sister can attend school,
So our village can ever greet the new year.
I stand here at the demarcation line
Looking South, remembering North.
I am divided like the land.

Postscript
After Xuan Diéu

To the River at Hien Luong
Ben Hai, between North and South
Unknown

> Translated by Keith Bosley

No Man's River, two months my friend
only today have I found the words
and still my heart chokes
   my lips taste bitter.
Tell me, river, how it is with you . . .

Over the awkward hill
down past the place of the old dynasty
through the villages
   I come to you
with tenderness, with love
and then with love, with longing go away.

No wider than a chopstick
   a peasant girl's halter
will bridge you, two banks reflecting
   her face and mine
no wider than this open palm!
Up at your source no banks divide:
down by the sea
   your mouth is no wider
   than a water carrier's yoke!
So wide this sadness
   this indignation
whose waves break endlessly on endless shores!

No Man's River, running blue below green trees
my heart goes out to you—
   what cramps it so?
Meeting, why is there parting in the eyes?
Two villages on either side of you
belong together as a body and its shadow:
what in heaven or on earth
   can change this?

Yet as I see them on the bank washing
the buffalo splashing about
    the coming and going
at blue noon the wide-eyed children
my eyes flood suddenly, my grip tightens:
I rip the unseen net apart
and gaze at them and gaze at them
I trample on the devils in the night
O my people
    and for a moment
this No Man's River
is the Perfumed River
is the Mekong
    swelling and swelling . . .

3

No Matter What We Do

WORK
David Huddle

I am a white, Episcopal-raised, almost
college-educated, North American male.
Sergeant Tri, my interpreter, is engrossed
in questioning our detainee, a small,
bad-smelling man in rags who claims to be
a farmer. I am filling in the blanks
of a form, writing down what Sergeant Tri
tells me. This is dull. Suddenly Tri yanks

our detainee to his feet, slaps him twice
across the bridge of his nose. The farmer
whimpers. Tri says the farmer has lied and waits
for orders. Where I grew up my father
waits at the door while my mother finishes
packing his lunch. I must tell Tri what next.

INTERROGATION
Dale Ritterbusch

A man sits in the afternoon,
crosslegged, arms tied behind to a stake;
the major is angry; that man knows, lies
about what he knows, plays dumb. The major
knows little of the language; his interpreter is bored.
The man is wasting the major's time;
there are lives at stake; there will be other prisoners,
other afternoons. "You VC!" "No! No VC!"
The major is impatient; he pulls out his knife,
plunges it into the thigh near the
prisoner's groin and rips down
to his knee. "You VC!" The major walks away.

PRISONER OF WAR

Michael Casey

5-11-198
Status: Civil Defendant
Le Thi Nguyet
VC nurse
Age: 17
ID#: Negative
Place of Capture: Tuyet Diem #4
Unit of Capture: B Co 5/46
Residence: Tuyet Diem #4

Subject stated she had been
Trained as a nurse at Tuyet
Diem #4. Training lasted 10
Days. Subject stated that she
Was chosen as there was a li-
Mited number of girls in her
Village. The training was gi-
Ven by a South Vietnamese wo-
Man, aged 24, whose name sub-
Ject did not know. Subject
Stated that at Tuyet Diem #4
Were four male medics whose
Names and ages she did not
Know but who never carried weapons.
Subject could not describe
The type of weapons which the
Male medics did not carry.
Subject was taught to change
Bandages and treat minor cuts
But was given no medical sup-
Plies upon completion of
Training. Subject did not know
Of VC/NVA activities in vicinity
Of her village. Subject will
Be sent to Binh Son for fur-
Ther interrogation by Vietna-
Mese National Police.

P.O.W.'s

R. L. Barth

Lieutenant Gilbert took us down the hill
This morning at first light, sweeping a ville
For sympathizers. I am guarding two
Of them, a mama-san and her child, who
Squat, fingers quick, blindfolded, loosely bound.
It's odd, but neither makes the smallest sound,
Kneading this silence that I cannot fill.

Sitting Still

Hoang Lien

Translated by Huynh Sanh Thong

Legs fastened to the thick brick floor
feel not the spinning earth.
I have sat still for two years at one spot,
night after night, the moon has waxed and waned.
In bunches, stars have faithfully bloomed
upon the trellis of thin prison bars,
A stillness for eternity,
untroubled by the flight of clouds.

In pain and sorrow I sit here,
silent and calm amidst the moon and stars.
No ocean's storm or hurricane
can move the hilltop high above.

I sit within all dirt and filth,
which moonlight filters off my soul.
Red dust is falling at the prison's door
But it can't stain the blue gown within

I sit within the cold and frost,
stoking the heart's true fire,
though flesh and bone may turn to stone,
like that lone woman with her child,
looking for him, her long-gone man,
waiting and waiting on a mountain peak.

Do You Know That, Inside the Cruel Jail

Nguyen Chi Thien

> *Translated by Huynh Sanh Thong*

Do you know that, inside the cruel jail,
unclothed, stark cold, with chattering teeth,
so starved that ribs will jut against the skin,
too ill and weak to put up any fight,
I stay awake through long white nights,
in silence making poems, O my friend?

Song from Prison

Ton That Lap

> *Translated by Don Luce, John Schafer, and Jacqui Chagnon*

Prison is a place
Where we train our wills.
It is a battle place
Where we need no weapons
Our hearts are made of steel
Which beat down the betrayer
Our blood is of bronze.
The blood we shed today
Will make tomorrow bright.

PASTORAL SCENE

Ho Chi Minh

Translated by Don Luce, John Schafer, and Jacqui Chagnon

When I came the rice was pale green.
Now it's cut in the barns.
Peasants laugh,
I hear them, here, across the rice fields.

ON THE WAY TO NANNING

Ho Chi Minh

Translated by Don Luce, John Schafer, and Jacqui Chagnon

The supple rope has now been replaced with iron fetters.
At every step they jingle like jade rings.
Though a prisoner, accused of being a spy,
I move with all the dignity of an ancient government official.

TUNG CHUN PRISON

Ho Chi Minh

Translated by Burton Raffel

Tung Chun prison, Ping Ma prison: the same thing,
Rice thin in tiny bowls, the stomach collapsed.
But at least there's water and light
And twice a day they open the bars and let the air in.

Reading the Poems of Ho

Daniel Berrigan

That cheerful attentiveness!
I am ashamed for my flaccid mind
that draws neither strength nor healing
from the springs of the world.
Prison; a 6-sided airless box, jerry built
Box, boxed, dimensions of death.

Yet today
earth burned like a bush
after a scourging night storm.
Midafternoon
a hawk, a cinquefoil, arose in the blue, straight up
at the east wall. He drank mid-distance
into his arched bonfire bones.
Torch, torch bearer, time's daemon. Below
the slow animal earth, lifting of prisoner's heads.

WE WERE PERMITTED TO MEET TOGETHER IN PRISON TO PREPARE FOR TRIAL

Daniel Berrigan

yesterday, the usual stiff-necked shakedown
room possessions person—then
entered the seemly company,
fellow indicted and co-conspirators.
nuns, priests, friends
the inadmissible evidence of their lives
vivid as blowing flowers in a dustbin
(the big eye outside, the praying mantis),
word went around quietly; we have bread and wine!
that unwinking eye
glassing over with boredom
the mice in all seriousness played
the Jesus game. a reading from Ezekiel
on the doomed city. Silence. Philip whispering over the bread
(a con, a magian), over the 'mt. dew' tin can.
we broke and passed the loaf, the furtive hands
of endangered animals.
my body given for you. my blood outpoured.
indictable action! as in the first instance
of vagrant Jesus, in whose flesh rumors and truth
collided; usual penalty, rigorously applied.

My friends, it is the savor of life
you passed to me; vines, the diminished loaf
lost hillsides where the sun
sets the grapes beating like a hive
of human hearts; Cornell gorges, the distant sea
Block Island swung like a hammock from its moorings—
I come to myself
a beast in a shoe box
sport
of the king of the cats

My Plight
(Sonnet: 1971–1972)

Norman A. McDaniel

As time goes by, I find no need to cry,
Though fate has frowned upon my upturned face,
And happiness has mostly passed me by,
I still await the hand of saving grace.

For six long years I've sat behind these bars,
Sometimes too cold, more often, though, too hot.
Through windows small at night I watch the stars
And wonder why to me befell this lot.

To cry would seem to say that I am weak,
Though six long years detained my strength has wrest;
While oft' from here my fate looks naught but bleak,
Still I must stand and try to meet the test.

I'm still a man and though I'm badly bent,
I'll hope and strive until my life is spent.

At a March Against the Vietnam War
Washington, November 27, 1965

Robert Bly

Newspapers rise high in the air over Maryland

We walk about, bundled in coats
    and sweaters in the late November sun

Looking down, I see feet moving

Calmly, gaily,
Almost as if separated from their bodies

But there is something moving in the dark somewhere
Just beyond
The edge of our eyes: a boat
Covered with machine guns
Moving along under the trees

It is black,
The hand reaches out
And cannot touch it—
It is that darkness among pine boughs
That the Puritans brushed
As they went out to kill turkeys

At the edge of the jungle clearing
It explodes
On the ground

We long to abase ourselves

We have carried around this cup of darkness
We have longed to pour it over our heads

We make war
Like a man anointing himself

UNCLE SAM AT THE PENTAGON
October 21, 1967

Jack Lindeman

Uncle Sam,
    why are you wearing a gas mask
        with the tiny tip
            of your white beard
                showing beneath it?
    And because you are shouldering a rifle
        to use against the most beautiful thing about you,
            your own soul,
                which is marching in unison against you today
                    (since it alone
                                    believes
                                    in your ultimate redemption),
    you are ugly beneath your iron helmet,
        ugly except for this minute harassment
            that seeks to unveil a mirror
                before your unhappy eyes.

The Distance

Denise Levertov

While we lie in the road to block traffic from the air-force
        base,
over there the dead are strewn in the roads.

While we are carried to the bus and off to jail to be 'processed,'
over there the torn-off legs and arms of the living
hang in burnt trees and on broken walls.

While we wait and sing in ugly but not unhabitable cells
men and women contorted, blinded, in tiger cages, are
            biting their tongues
to stifle, for each other's sake, their cries of agony.
And those cruel cages are built in America.

While we refuse the standard prison liverwurst sandwiches,
knowing we'll get decent food in a matter of hours,
over there free fighters, young and old, guns never laid aside,
eat a few grains of rice and remember
Uncle Ho, and the long years he ate no better, and smile.

And while we fear
for the end of earth-life, even though we sing
and rejoice in each other's beauty and comradeship,

over there they mourn
the dead and mutilated each has seen.

They have seen and seen and heard and heard
all that we will ourselves with such effort to imagine,
to summon into understanding . . .
And they too sing.
They too rejoice
in each other's beauty and comradeship.

They sing and fight. I see their spirits
visible, crowns of fire-thorn
flicker over their heads.

Our steps toward struggle
are like the first tottering of infant feet.

Could we,

        if life lasts,

                find in ourselves

that steady courage, win
such flame-crowns?

MAY 1968

Sharon Olds

When the Dean said we could not cross campus
until the students gave up the buildings,
we lay down, in the street,
we said the cops will enter this gate
over us. Lying back on the cobbles,
I saw the buildings of New York City
from dirt level, they soared up
and stopped, chopped off—above them, the sky,
the night air over the island.
The mounted police moved, near us,
while we sang, and then I began to count,
12, 13, 14, 15,
I counted again, 15, 16, one
month since the day on that deserted beach,
17, 18, my mouth fell open,
my hair on the street,
if my period did not come tonight
I was pregnant. I could see the sole of a cop's
shoe, the gelding's belly, its genitals—
if they took me to Women's Detention and did
the exam on me, the speculum,
the fingers—I gazed into the horse's tail
like a comet-train. All week, I had
thought about getting arrested, half-longed
to give myself away. On the tar—
one brain in my head, another,
in the making, near the base of my tail—
I looked at the steel arc of the horse's
shoe, the curve of its belly, the cop's

nightstick, the buildings streaming up
away from the earth. I knew I should get up
and leave, but I lay there looking at the space
above us, until it turned deep blue and then
ashy, colorless, *Give me this one*
night, I thought, *and I'll give this child*
the rest of my life, the horses' heads,
this time, drooping, dipping, until
they slept in a circle around my body and my daughter.

Fifteenth Day of the Fourth Month of the Year 1972

L. Russell Herman Jr.

We called it
Resistance Day
and a bunch of us
gathered downtown
at the state capitol building
to make public
our acts of resistance to the war.
It was a small group
maybe twenty or twenty-five.
One by one members of the group
rose up from the grass
and walked to the microphone
and, speaking through the mike to the crowd,
told
  their name
  and their method of resistance
  and a little bit about why.

When they told their names
they were the names of real people,
  friends,
  citizens
  neighbors,
  close friends,
  good folks.

When they told of their resistance
they spoke of
   refusing to pay income taxes to buy death
      and refusing to pay the phone tax which was levied to
buy war
      and refusing to collaborate with the draft.

When they told of why
they spoke of
   their god
   their conscience
   the friends they left in Vietnam
      when they were there to kill
      both American and Vietnamese friends
   the planes and troops on alert here at home in our own
state
   the faceless bureaucracy that demands their money or
their life
   a two-year-old son
   our heritage of life, liberty and pursuit of happiness
   courts that do not allow arguments about morality or
conscience
And then one of my friends
(who as a child had barely escaped the Gestapo)
pointed out to us
the flowering dogwood trees
      around us like white puffs of smoke
and the red azaleas
      like cool fire licking at the building
and then my friend spoke of
she spoke
of white phosphorus
      which burns for a week in the flesh of a child
and of
      falling fire from the sky which consumes villages.

Tonight on the TV it was announced that they have bombed
Haiphong.
No matter what we do, it is not yet enough.

May, 1972

James Schuyler

Soft May mists are here again.
There, the war goes on.
Beside the privet the creamy
white tulips are extra
fine this year. There,
foliage curls blackened back:
it will, it must
return. But when?
A cardinal enchants me
with its song.
All war is wrong. The grass
here is green and buttoned
down with dandelions. A car
goes by. What peace. It—
the war—goes on. Fleeing
people. The parrot tulips
look like twisted guts.
Blood on green.
Here, a silent scream.
Can we, in simple justice,
desert our sought allies?
Draw out: I do not know.
I know the war is wrong.
We have it in us
to triumph over hate and
death, or so
the suburban spring suggests.
Here, the drive is wet
with mist. There,
the war goes on. Children
are more valuable than
flowers: what a choice
to make! The war
must end. It goes on.

ON BEING ASKED TO WRITE A POEM AGAINST THE WAR IN VIETNAM

Hayden Carruth

Well I have and in fact
more than one and I'll
tell you this too

I wrote one against
Algeria that nightmare
and another against

Korea and another
against the one
I was in

and I don't remember
how many against
the three

when I was a boy
Abyssinia Spain and
Harlan County

and not one
breath was restored
to one

shattered throat
mans womans or childs
not one not

one
but death went on and on
never looking aside

except now and then like a child
with a furtive half-smile
to make sure I was noticing.

THIS WAR
May 1972

Philip Levine

You go down to the grave
and pound on the roof
until the woman answers,
the child cries, until
the man in his coat of fire
opens and you enter
the charred eye flaking
into white streams, the voice
howling in the darkened subway,
the teeth grinding stones,
until a new wind
stirs the thumbs of onions
and the purple chives scatter
on the grass and the wren
comes back.

The lights
of the slaughter house
burn all day.
No one comes. The old mare
waits in the bricked alley
her loose flesh sliding
against flies. She sees
the cloud pass over
the sun and break against
the mountains. You
turn to the foothills
where the day walks
through birch leaves lifting
in surprise.

Or no one hears.
Your knees bang down
on the bare floor,
your forehead opens
and the secrets spill out

like mud. No one answers.
The mouth of the grave
closes, the tongue lopped
off at the root, and the last
word comes down
this spring day, pale ashes
overflowing the basin
of Los Angeles, a scum
on the sea of tears
coming down.

AMERICA: DECEMBER 1972

Don Luce

The children
Have poured into the streets
Of our cities and villages
Students with hope for tomorrow
Join their grandparents' tiny tottering steps
To march, to sing, to stop the war

There comes a time
Writes Denise Levertov, the poet
When anger is the only love
And America debates the killing
Where do we channel our love
Dear friend Denise
Where?

Richard Nixon is the enemy
Not the people of Grinnell
Shout the angry students
On the evening of Nixon's
        declaration
        of war
        on the peoples of the world

Seven hundred
March at 2:00 a.m. that night
At Grinnell

A quiet flickering of candles
As defenseless and as
        strong as Gandhi
        with his spinning wheel

Peace Now!
Wrote the students at Drake
On the sidewalks of their campus
And were charged with
        Malicious
        Destruction
        Of Property
While Richard, the King
Dropped napalm on the
        children of Vietnam

Irresponsible dissent!
Cried ministers from their pulpits
Long-haired hippie radicals
Shouted politicians
Giving Fourth of July speeches
Months too early

We have become a dangerous country
Says Dan Ellsberg
Now charged with treason
For proving
Our country's leaders have been lying
For ten long years

Yes, out of this sea of anger/love
Respect for children will come
The bombing will stop
Because the children of America
        will no longer
        push the buttons
        that drop the bombs
        for Mr. Kissinger and
        Mr. Nixon.

ON HEARING A NEW ESCALATION

Richard Hugo

From time one I've been reading slaughter,
seeing the same bewildered face of a child
staring at nothing beside his dead mother
in Egypt, the pyramid blueprints approved,
the phrases of national purpose streaming
from the mouth of some automated sphinx.
Day on day, the same photographed suffering,
the bitterness, the opportune hate handed down
from Xerxes to Nixon, a line strong
as transatlantic cable and stale ideals.
Killing's still in though glory is out of style.
And what does it come to, this blood cold
in the streets and a history book printed
and bound with such cost saving American
methods, the names and dates are soon bones?
Beware certain words: Enemy. Liberty. Freedom.
Believe those sounds and you're aiming a bomb.

4

Still the War Goes On

My Beloved Is Dead in Vietnam

For Trinh Cong Son, author of The Mad Woman

Thuong Vuong-Riddick

> *Dark or blue, all beloved, all beautiful.*
> *Numberless eyes have seen the day.*
> *They sleep in the grave,*
> *and the sun still rises.*
> > —*Sully Prudhomme*

My beloved is
Dead in Diên Biên Phu
Dead in Lao Kay, dead in Cao Bang
Dead in Langson, dead in Mong Cai
Dead in Thai Nguyên, dead in Hanoï
Dead in Haïphong, dead in Phat Diêm
Dead in Ninh-Binh, dead in Thanh Hoa
Dead in Vinh, dead in Hatinh
Dead in Hue, dead in Danang, dead in Quang Tri
Dead in Quang Ngai, dead in Qui Nhon
Dead in Kontum, dead in Pleiku
Dead in Dalat, dead in Nha-Tranh
Dead in My Tho, dead in Tuy Hoa
Dead in Biên Hoa, dead in Ban Me Thuot
Dead in Tayninh, dead in Anloc
Dead in Saigon, dead in Biên Hoa
Dead in Can Tho, dead in Soc Trang

Vietnam, how many times
I have wanted to call your name
I have forgotten
the human sound.

Dead

Mark Kessinger

We had every kind of death in Nam,
fast dead, near dead,
fuckin dead,
point blank dead,
blown away dead
unconfirmed dead
confirmed dead
missing presumed dead
wish I was home or dead
dead warmed over
walking dead
dead head
living dead
next to dead
in line for dead
deadheads
dead ends,
it's a word you get
tired of
after a while
but you learn to
live with it
in spite of yourself
part of the landscape
part of the dead you live among.

Love Song of a Woman Maddened by the War

Trinh Cong Son

Translated by Don Luce, John Schafer, and Jacqui Chagnon

I had a lover who died at the battle of Pleime,
I had a lover who died at Battle Zone "D,"
Who died at Dong Xoai,
Who died at Hanoi,
He died far away on the distant frontier.

I had a lover who died in the battle of Chu Prong,
I had a lover whose body drifted along a river,
Who died in the dark forest,
Whose charred body lies cold and abandoned.

I want to love you, love Viet Nam,
The day when the wind is strong
I whisper your name and the name of Viet Nam,
We are so close, the same voice and yellow race.
I want to love you, love Viet Nam,
But as soon as I grow up my ears are accustomed
To the sound of bullets and mines;
My hands are now free but I forget from now on the human
     language.

I had a lover who died at Ashau,
I had a lover whose twisted body lies in a valley,
Who died under a bridge, naked and voiceless.
I had a lover who died at the battle of Ba Gia,
I had a lover who died just last night,
He passed away in a dream with no feelings of hate.

CAMBODIA

James Fenton

One man shall smile one day and say goodbye.
Two shall be left, two shall be left to die.

One man shall give his best advice.
Three men shall pay the price.

One man shall live, live to regret.
Four men shall meet the debt.

One man shall wake from terror to his bed.
Five men shall be dead.

One man to five. A million men to one.
And still they die. And still the war goes on.

LAOS

David Widup

The *Stars and Stripes* says
"Nixon promises no war in Laos!"

I stand in the Aerial Port,
on my way to Nah Trang,
and there's a line of grunts
a mile long,
a snake full of killing evil,
waiting in line.

I've never seen a line like this,
in eleven months,
and ask a friendly looking,
blond grunt,
"What's happening?"
He says,
"Laos"
and spits at my feet,
looks the other way
so I know he's had enough
of talking about the War.

They all died.
Every one of them died,
before anyone knew they were there.

BUTTER

Tom V. Schmidt

Today at the Gateway
to the Pacific
Travis AFB California
we loaded a cattle
truck full with
bodies fresh off
the plane from Con Thien.

Vacuum sealed in
smooth extrusions as
shiny and neat
as your latest poptop
beer can:

**Container, Cadaver
Aluminum, PROS 1467, Reusable**

**Nomenclature of Contents
The human remains of
Transportation #757XOD3967 Cpl E4**

(or some kind
of sergeant once
that weighed 143 lbs. net.)

Tarp over to protect
motorists from the glare
on the highway
to Oakland the truck
pulled out and we watched
silent
   wiping wet palms
on our green thighs.

Soldier's Widow: A Generic Photo

Fran Castan

The widow always wears a black coat.
She is cold in this coat even in summer.
She is here to receive the flag.
She is here to say hers is a small sacrifice
for God and for country. Valium
is the drug of choice for such occasions.
She will not cry out. She will not collapse.
Two men, solid as a pair of bookends,
flank her and grip her arms.
They wear dark suits or other uniforms.
"Hero" is the theme of the eulogy,
as if her husband chose to give his life.
Tonight, she will sleep with the widow's quilt,
the folded flag taken from his coffin.

Thirteen

Le Minh Thu, age thirteen
> *Translated by Don Luce, John Schafer, and Jacqui Chagnon*

Once mother told me.
"You were born in the Year of the Dog
And when the next Year of the Dog comes
You will be thirteen and strong enough
To help your father in the rice fields."

Now I am thirteen
But have seen no dogs in our village:
"They would disturb the guerillas at night,"
My mother said, softly.

Nor have I seen my father:
"He gave his life for the mountains and rivers of Viet Nam."
My mother said, weeping.

PEACE

Thich Nhat Hanh

They woke me this morning
to tell me my brother had been killed in battle.
Yet in the garden
a new rose, with moist petals uncurling,
blooms on the bush.
And I am alive,
still breathing the fragrance of roses and dung,
eating, praying, and sleeping.
When can I break my long silence?
When can I speak the unuttered words that are choking me?

LETTER FROM NAM

for my brother, Verne

Sharon Lee

On June 10, 1969
eight days ago
you were alive.

Your hand
moved across these pages.

Your flesh was intact
your young heart
was beating,
there was life
in your body
on June 10.

> We who sit and wait
> pull the minutes apart
> between newscasts
> the daily death toll
> and letters.

Eight days ago
you wore a helmet
with a peace sign

sprouting flowers.
You posed for this
polaroid with two
Vietnamese children
the three of you
calling time out
to send me a sign
of peace, their
chubby fingers
recording this
day in history
June 10, 1969.

For Timothy Clover

Liz Farrell

Few know a death's precise day and hour and minute,
the knowledge that freezes sundials.

                              One froze
at 1:28 A.M. on the 22nd of May 1968 in Vietnam
when Timothy, soldier, poet, husband, father was shot
dead. Heaven cannot hold all of him:

                              Scraps
of paper, unfinished poems found in his pockets,
float unseen on every wind, float
on in all their immense weight . . .
Sometime Timothy's bullet-holed, blood-
soaked pieces of poetry must weigh as much on this nation
as body counts of our nameless men.

                              I met you, Timothy,
when David read your poems, Davy, your good buddy, your
pallbearer and troubadour who reads you back to life.
All who listen see your vision focus in Vietnamese
landscapes: mountains made crooked under napalmed
caps, laughter gouged out of children, women whose
bodies are joyless as mortar, "that whirlybirdman
. . . colliding with a butterfly . . ."

Weep . . .
for what Timothy told is buried in the dreams-turned
nightmare of a generation of innocent G.I.'s who know
him in their scarred sleep.

My country's soldiers, I see
you rise in the West, assembled at the port that shipped
you out. I see you march, a funeral procession for Timothy,
march until you crumble every power at the wheels that drive
this war and stoke the next.

In the wake
grow sweet fields of timothy grass.
Rest In Peace.

A MOTHER'S EVENING MEDITATION

Minh Dung

Translated by Nguyen Ngoc Bich, Burton Raffel, and W. S. Merwin

I fill a bowl with new rice
place ebony chopsticks at the side
chase the flies away
and often I see your face as it looked
the last time you came home.

Today the fields looked ripe,
the empty train came back
spouting black smoke above warm grass.

I fill this bowl to the edge, place ebony
chopsticks at the side and chase
the flies away. Today is the end
of the month, you would be getting paid today
if you were alive.
You would be going downtown, smoking,
sending postcards home.

I fill the bowl with new rice
look at the pair of chopsticks and your son,
just fallen asleep.
A wonderful child, peaceful as a pebble,

he is half-a-year-old now but still has no name.
This is your anniversary.
Suddenly your wife holds her head and cries—
"He died in his spring!"

I fill a bowl with new rice
and sit, noticing the signs of autumn, the fallen leaves . . .
The child in the cradle smiles at me
I place the ebony chopsticks
chase the flies away
and wipe the streaming tears.

Luom

To Huu
> *Translated by Keith Bosley*

Back in blood-hot Hue
uncle from Hanoi
unexpectedly
meets nephew in street:

nephew tiny, tiny
bag little, little
feet nimble, nimble
head cocked to one side

cap at an angle
mouth whistles loudly
singing like a bird
hops on yellow road.

"I'm a runner now—
very smart, uncle.
I'd much rather be
in camp than at home."

Nephew laughs two slits
cheeks red as date plums:
"Right. Goodbye, comrade!"
Nephew goes away.

Nephew goes own way:
uncle where he came.
Now in the sixth month
there is news from home.

That's how it is, Luom.

One of these fine days
like any other
little comrade puts
letters in his bag

crosses battlefield
shells wow-wowing by
letters marked URGENT
fearless of danger

empty country road
the paddy in bloom
the little lad's cap
bobs above the field.

A sudden red flash
and there it is, Luom:
the little comrade
a stream of fresh blood.

On rice lies nephew
hand tight round a stem
of sweet-smelling rice.
Soul flits over fields.

Luom, what is there left?

Nephew tiny, tiny
bag little, little
feet nimble, nimble
head cocked to one side

cap at an angle
mouth whistles loudly
singing like a bird
hops on yellow road.

The Skull Beside a Mountain Trail

(Kui Ky Lan, September 1969)

Frank Cross

Quietly, intently
We slipped down
The canopied mountain trail.
Suddenly, we were startled
By a skull,
Perched upright, beside the trail.
The skull appeared ancient,
But probably only months
Had passed since a brain
Within this bone,
Worried about its safety.

5

Asia Is in Flames

Untitled
Dick Shea

marine sitting in the position of supreme contentment
on a wooden box with a hole in it
covering a hole in the ground
unsunburned part of his body exposed
head resting on fist
gazing to sea
traffic going by behind him
a playboy magazine beside him
with some of the less important pages missing
picture of tranquility
would make a good photograph
entitled the war in vietnam

Shitbirds
Jon Forrest Glade

One of the most disgusting duties
you could get in Vietnam
was the shitburning detail.
Defecation from the latrines
was collected in the bottom halves
of fifty gallon drums,
then taken somewhere near
or outside the perimeter,
doused with diesel fuel
and set on fire.
I didn't really mind doing that;
it was an activity that officers
and non-coms
didn't like to get too close to,
and the stench definitely covered
the smell of marijuana.
Besides, I always thought of the contents
of those flaming barrels
as burned offerings
to the gods
of that particular war.

Burning Shit at An Khe

Bruce Weigl

Into that pit
   I had to climb down
with a rake and matches; eventually,
   you had to do something
because it just kept piling up
   and it wasn't our country, it wasn't
our air thick with the sick smoke
   so another soldier and I
lifted the shelter off its blocks
   to expose the homemade toilets:
fifty-five-gallon drums cut in half
   with crude wood seats that splintered.
We soaked the piles in fuel oil
   and lit the stuff
and tried to keep the fire burning.
   To take my first turn
I paid some kid
   a CARE package of booze from home.
I'd walked past the burning once
   - and gagged the whole heart of myself—
it smelled like the world
   - was on fire,
but when my turn came again
   there was no one
so I stuffed cotton up my nose
   and marched up that hill. We poured
and poured until it burned and black
   smoke curdled
but the fire went out.
   Heavy artillery
hammered the evening away in the distance,
   Vietnamese laundry women watched
from a safe place, laughing.
   I'd grunted out eight months
of jungle and thought I had a grip on things
   but we flipped the coin and I lost

and climbed down into my fellow soldiers'
    shit and began to sink and didn't stop
until I was deep to my knees. Liftships
    cut the air above me, the hacking
blast of their blades
    ripped dust in swirls so every time
I tried to light a match
    it died
and it all came down on me, the stink
    and the heat and the worthlessness
until I slipped and climbed
    out of that hole and ran
past the olive-drab
    tents and trucks and clothes and everything
green as far from the shit
    as the fading light allowed.
Only now I can't fly.
    I lay down in it
and fingerprint the words of who I am
    across my chest
until I'm covered and there's only one smell,
    one word.

THE LAST DETAIL

Leroy V. Quintana

In the boonies with Charlie
trying to blow your shit away
for a year.
You came out
and the Army had one last detail:
Had you burning the shit of the Vietnamese workers
in cut-off fifty-five gallon drums.

SHORT TIMER

Doug Anderson

Twelve hours before his plane was to lift off for home
he was sitting in the EM club
slugging down Filipino beer.
A sniper round rang through the tin roof,
knocked him off his stool, a near complete flip
before he hit the floor.
Next thing I knew we were lugging him
through the sand toward the sick bay;
him bucking and screaming,
me trying to shield the spurting head,
the sniper bearing down on us,
the others scattering to the perimeter to return fire.
Inside we saw how bad it was.
I syringed the long gash in the parietal with sterile water,
the doctor with a flashlight looking close,
the man saying, *Oh God,* and already the slur,
the drool. He would live. Go home.
Sit the rest of his life in front of a television set.
Back in the EM club they had wiped up the blood
and we could see the stars
through the thirty caliber holes in the roof.
What was in the 20 cc's of brain he lost?
These are the things that can occupy a drunk about to black
        out.
Somewhere a family, a girlfriend, prepared for his return.
Somewhere a telegram raced toward them into Pacific Time
and the dark that rose like water in his room.

A Drinking Song

Tran Da Tu
Translated by Huynh Sanh Thong

We have two arms—
what good, though, are two arms?
What can they hug today?

We have two legs—
what good, though, are two legs?
Our homeland is no longer home.

We have two ears—
what good, though, are two ears?
Bullets and bombs are shrieking now.

We have two eyes—
what good, though, are two eyes?
Night follows night, drags on and on.

We have two nostrils—
what good, though, are two nostrils?
Flowers and leaves have withered up.

We have a throat—
what good, though, is a throat?
Our breath has lost all warmth.

We have a mouth—
what good, though, is a mouth?
We can no longer give a cry.

The liquor's going flat—
please raise your cup, my friends.

HAIRCUT
David Huddle

open shop on the strip: Vietnamese barber
standing up is not quite as tall as GI
sitting down, but very serious, scampers
around, snips those scissors, raises them high
over GI's head as if GI had hair
longer than a quarter of an inch to start
with and this was a *salon* in Paris
instead of a shack with no walls and a dirt

floor. At the end he carefully clips hairs
from GI's nose, inserts two small hollow
bamboo sticks in GI's ears, twists them on each
side to ream out the wax, then twangs the sticks. Holds
GI's head, limbers the neck, pops it, scares
GI. Could have died then. 25 p. please.

UNTITLED
Dick Shea

went to a barbershop today
three walls
6 by 6
made of pressed beer cans cardboard
and corrugated metal roof
it held a waiting bench and a chair
the barber came from another house
with mirror and well worn equipment
he covered me with a dirty sheet
clipped with hand clippers
and broken scissors
trimmed with slicing razor
threw powder in my face
soaked head in some odd tasting eye smarting oil
took my 30 piastres (20¢)
and laughed

as i went away bald
while i had him shave me to whiteness
a crowd of kids gathered
they called me captain buddha

ON WHAT THE ARMY DOES WITH HEADS

Michael Casey

Most Americans like kids
GI's is no exception
They likes to play with kids
Walking up to them
Pattin them on the head
Hey ya cute lit fucker
Now
If you see a little bald-headed kid
Don't do that
Don't go pattin him on the head
This kid's Buddhist
An it's against his religion
You do that
An to them
To these people here
You've fucked with the kid's head
An no one can
Convince that kid's mama
You didn do it on purpose

THE MOON IN CIRCLES OF FLAME

Pham Tien Duat

Translated by Nguyen Quang Thieu and Kevin Bowen

Delayed-action bombs rip up the hilltop.
The sky is mottled in red circles of flame.
Through the explosions, I watch
the moon rise straight up from the crest of the hill.

Trees sway under the lightning's flash.
By the guard station engineers
sit and rest. A young soldier sings.
He knows a young woman is listening in a nearby trench.

Shadowed in canvas, trucks tumble
down through the lightning. Over the hill
a moon burns red
in circling fires.

Friends, the engineers are deep and quiet men.
The smell of cordite hangs in the chords of their song.
The hail of the marble bombs will taper, the rain
of shrapnel on our helmets will grow weak.

Along the road all night I hear the whisper, whisper,
the soil's veins merging, my country's two halves joining.
I see the halo of the moon, my country
rising higher and higher through the circling fire.

THE ASIANS DYING

W. S. Merwin

When the forests have been destroyed their darkness remains
The ash the great walker follows the possessors
Forever
Nothing they will come to is real
Nor for long
Over the watercourses
Like ducks in the time of the ducks
The ghosts of the villages trail in the sky
Making a new twilight

Rain falls into the open eyes of the dead
Again again with its pointless sound
When the moon finds them they are the color of everything

The nights disappear like bruises but nothing is healed
The dead go away like bruises
The blood vanishes into the poisoned farmlands
Pain the horizon
Remains
Overhead the seasons rock
They are paper bells
Calling to nothing living

The possessors move everywhere under Death their star
Like columns of smoke they advance into the shadows
Like thin flames with no light
They with no past
And fire their only future

BURNING THE NEWS

Lewis Turco

The fire is eating
the paper. The child who drowned
is burned. Asia is in flames.
As he signs his great
bill, a minister of state chars

at the edges and curls
into smoke. The page rises,
glowing, over the neighbor's
roof. In the kitchens
clocks turn, pages turn like gray wings,

slowly, over armchairs.
Another child drowns, a bill
is signed, and the pen blackens.
The smoke of Asia
drifts among the neighbors like mist.

It is a good day for burning.
The fire is eating the news.

It Is Dangerous to Read Newspapers

Margaret Atwood

While I was building neat
castles in the sandbox,
the hasty pits were
filling with bulldozed corpses

and as I walked to the school
washed and combed, my feet
stepping on the cracks in the cement
detonated red bombs.

Now I am grownup
and literate, and I sit in my chair
as quietly as a fuse

and the jungles are flaming, the under-
brush is charged with soldiers,
the names on the difficult
maps go up in smoke.

I am the cause, I am a stockpile of chemical
toys, my body
is a deadly gadget,
I reach out in love, my hands are guns,
my good intentions are completely lethal.

Even my
passive eyes transmute
everything I look at to the pocked
black and white of a war photo,
how
can I stop myself

It is dangerous to read newspapers.

Each time I hit a key
on my electric typewriter,
speaking of peaceful trees

another village explodes.

WATCHING THE NEWS

Paul Martin

From out there, the news keeps coming
focusing here in front of the couch:
    mountains of shoes and eyeglasses;
    the limousine turning the corner, forward,
    backward, slowed down, enlarged, and stopped;
    that naked girl running toward me,
    her back aflame with napalm—
these pictures that make it difficult to mow the lawn
to replace a burned out bulb or the brick

above the door where the starling returns each year
to build her nest. For weeks I watched her carry
each strand and now the eggs have hatched
on a narrow ledge inside the wall.
Though I can't see their blind eyes, their stretching necks
I can hear them as soon as she enters the hole.
      Last year
trying their wings toward the light, they tipped
the nest deeper into the wall.
At night I could hear their faint chirping
from somewhere near the bottom.
I promised then I'd repair that hole,
but here it is another Spring
and the starling continues to fly out and in
dropping food into the silence
and I can feel my chances piling up
like small, delicate bones in the darkness.

"You and I Are Disappearing"

—Björn Håkansson

Yusef Komunyakaa

The cry I bring down from the hills
belongs to a girl still burning
inside my head. At daybreak
   she burns like a piece of paper.
She burns like foxfire
in a thigh-shaped valley.
A skirt of flames
dances around her
at dusk.
   We stand with our hands
hanging at our sides,
while she burns
   like a sack of dry ice.
She burns like oil on water.
She burns like a cattail torch
dipped in gasoline.
She glows like the fat tip
of a banker's cigar,
   silent as quicksilver.
A tiger under a rainbow
     at nightfall.
She burns like a shot glass of vodka.
She burns like a field of poppies
at the edge of a rain forest.
She rises like dragonsmoke
   to my nostrils.
She burns like a burning bush
driven by a godawful wind.

The Body Burning Detail

Bill Jones

Three soldiers from the North
Burned for reasons
Of sanitation.
Arms shrunk to seal flippers
Charred buttocks thrust skyward
They burned for five days.
It was hard to swallow
Difficult to eat
With the sweet smoke of seared
Flesh, like fog,
Everywhere.

Twenty-five years later
They burn still.
Across seas of time
The faint unwelcome odor
Rises in odd places.
With a load of leaves
At the city dump
A floating wisp of smoke
From the burning soldiers
Mingles with the stench
Of household garbage.

Once, while watching young boys
Kick a soccer ball,
The Death Smell filled my lungs.
As I ran, choking
Panic unfolded
Fluttering wings
Of fear and remorse.
A narrow escape.

A letter, snatched from flames
The day we burned them
Is hidden away
In a shoebox

With gag birthday cards,
Buttons, string, rubber bands.
A letter from home?
The Oriental words,
Delicately formed,
Are still a mystery.

6

They Will Not Cry

Vietnam #4

Clarence Major

a cat said
on the corner

the other day
dig man

how come so many
of us
niggers

are dying over there
in that white
man's war

they say more of us
are dying

than them peckerwoods
& it just
    don't make sense

unless it's true
that the honkeys

are trying to kill us out
with the same stone

they killing them other cats
with

you know, he said
two birds with one stone

Report from the Skull's Diorama

Yusef Komunyakaa

Dr. King's photograph
comes at me from *White Nights*
like Hoover's imagination at work,

dissolving into a scenario
at Firebase San Juan Hill:
our chopper glides in closer,
down to the platoon of black GIs
back from night patrol

with five dead. Down
into a gold whirl of leaves
dust-deviling the fire base.
A field of black trees
stakes down the morning sun.

With the chopper blades
knife-fighting the air,
yellow leaflets quiver
back to the ground, clinging to us.
These men have lost their tongues,

but the red-bordered
leaflets tell us
VC didn't kill
Dr. Martin Luther King.
The silence etched into their skin

is also mine. Psychological
warfare colors the napalmed hill
gold-yellow. When our gunship
flies out backwards, rising
above the men left below

to blend in with the charred
landscape, an AK-47
speaks, with the leaflets
clinging to the men & stumps,
waving to me across the years.

A Negro Soldier's Viet Nam Diary

Herbert Woodward Martin

The day he discovered a mother and child in the river, he
wrote:

They had been there a month; the water had begun to tear
them apart.
The mother had not relaxed, even in death she held to her
child.
I lowered my gun slowly into the water, walked away.
My stomach screamed empty, there was nothing there.
What little warm water I had would not Pilot away the mud
or stench.
It was like a dead body we could not discover.
Death hangs on the rice.
The ground is watered with blood.
The land bears no fruit.
Grass is an amenity.
It is a luxury forever to notice so much as a flower,
Or clear water in a stream.
Bullets, here, kill with the same deliberate speed that they do
at home.
Fear destroys the thing it is unacquainted with.
I never want to kill again.
Do not celebrate me when and if I come home.
I step around the smallest creature these days.
I am cautious to pray.
I am cautious to believe the day will come when we can
Take up our sharing again with deliberate speed.
Have you prayed, lately, for that?

Ballade of the Saigon Streets

Herbert Krohn

Tu Do is the loveliest of all the Saigon streets.
From Church of Our Lady to bars of our soldiers
are blossoms that fall at the pleasure of the wind.
Whores and the Virgin are *Tu Do*'s tourist pleasures.
They have suffered before us and they will not cry.

Trinh Minh The is Soulville, the Saigon River street
where sepia girls, dark streets, and Negro soldiers
float in marijuana clouds that sweeten the wind.
French-African souvenirs born out of pleasure,
these girls suffered before us and they will not cry.

Continental Cafe, not far from *Le Loi* Street—
Maugham drank with the French here, alcoholic soldiers
whose battles are now dreams, whose ghosts dwell on the
        wind
their hell. War was their sin and Cognac their pleasure
when they suffered before us but they did not cry.

Prince, tourist, Christian soldier, seize the Saigon streets
that flower before you with their varied pleasures.
Unlike the wind and city, you live only once.
They have suffered before you and they will not cry.

Cicada Song

Christian Nguyen Langworthy

Nights when the women are out,
        the children asleep,
the soldiers walk about the streets.
Nights when you hear the loud talk
        and drunken bouts,
        the cicadas weep.

The Women Next Door

Barbara Tran

Whenever Mother was out at the market
or inside praying, we'd sneak up to the railing.
I could never tell if the women in the courtyard
were trying to break away, but their cries
always seemed pained and they were always
on the bottom, as if hiding their bodies
under the large, pale American men.

The women knew my brothers
and I often crouched at the railing,
peering farther over the edge
with each cry, on to the open courtyard.
Once, I met Hien's eyes. She withdrew
under the body above her, quickly as a reflex,
her hair snaking under the dingy sheet.
She stayed quiet for minutes after our eyes met.
I was frozen in that spot, watching
the soldier fight her harder and harder.
The cot rocked and creaked, the women
around, joining in its cries. Slowly,
I backed up against the wall, stood,
ran away.

My brothers and I wanted to know
what these soldiers were paying for.
We saw them, the younger ones
line up at the front door on certain days,
money in hand. The older ones
were surer, patting all the men
in the village on the head, no matter
what their age. They'd boom
their greetings and swing a girl
or two into their chests before the door
closed and we couldn't see anymore.
Then we'd run up to the terrace
on the 2nd floor, just as the men
emerged into the courtyard, drink
in hand, woman leading them to a bed.

This was when they'd get louder, more
demanding, pride or shame swelling up.
We'd sink down low, watch the women,
who were already naked. The men could
think of nothing but themselves as the women
undid their buttons and zippers, stroking
and cooing like new mothers. But once
the men were naked and in bed, the women
looked elsewhere, mostly up, as if someone
might save them. But there were only
us kids, peering down with hope in our eyes
that the women wouldn't call out for Mother.
Strangely, they seemed thankful to us, as if
our company somehow comforted them
even as they lay in American arms.
They never once offered us money
or any American T-shirts or anything else
the men left behind, but sometimes
when Mother wasn't home and they didn't
have any company, Hien would call me over.
We'd sit on her doorstep, and she'd comb
my hair. These were the only times
I looked at her straight on. Whenever she
was in the courtyard, laughing and carrying on,
I'd call my brothers away. She never once
tried to buy me with chocolate or Bic pens.
It was only her smile and her hands
on my shoulders.

Even as I Lie Pretending Sleep
Christian Nguyen Langworthy

Even as I lie pretending sleep
to deceive you into believing
I will not know the presence

of that man pressed against your bosom;
even as I catch you both watching
with amusement my innocent sleep

to ensure I will not see or hear
the moments of your entanglement;
even as I lie pretending sleep,

this house shivers in its worry
to the wind; how the shutters knock
in stuttering voices to register

complaints about your limbs entwined,
and I think of all the nights devised—
the price exacted for the hours spent

exchanging favors under linen sheets;
and even as your son pretends to sleep
his eyelids, closed, could never be dams

against the tide and flow of tears
when in the hours those men revisited.

A Black Soldier Remembers:
Horace Coleman/Shaka Aku Shango

My Saigon Daughter I saw only once,
standing in the dusty square across
from the Brink BOQ/PX, in back of
the National Assembly, not far from the
ugly statue of the crouching marines facing
the fish pond the VC blew up during Tet.

The amputee beggars watch us.
The girl and I have the same color
and the same eyes.

She does not offer me one of
the silly hats she offers Americans
but I'm not Senegalese and
I have nothing she needs but
the sad smile she already has.

Bui Doi 2

R. A. Streitmatter/Tran Trong Dat

She looked upon the small infant,
Large eyes, same arched eyebrows.
Content, engulfed within her strong arms
And she could not speak.

She questioned, hoped that the newborn would understand
By some telepathic maternal bridge
That which needed to be understood, to be felt, to be said.
She said
My son, with my eyes and with my heart,
Grow to be a strong, proud and able man.
She said
Look upon me with your large dark curious eyes
And remember . . .

Only now I can't remember and I can't understand
Why she left me in a basket on the steps of a Saigon
    orphanage.
I cannot fathom her actual pain, only the residual pain,
Her only legacy to me, the loss impaling my soul.

THE SADNESS
Bill Shields

little Amerasian kids
panhandling the streets
for smokes
candy
c-rats

they knew death like fatherly love

those absent
vacant
eyes

all too ready to die

SONS WITHOUT FATHERS
Christian Nguyen Langworthy

Sons without fathers sleep in meager light,
in dim consequences within
the dark rooms of night.
When growing older, they come to terms
with demons hardly aged;
they learn to fight
the wars their fathers waged.

Ok Corral East

Brothers in the Nam

Horace Coleman/Shaka Aku Shango

Sgt Christopher and I are in Khanh Hoi,
down by the docks in the Blues Bar.
The women are brown and there is no "Saigon Tea."
We're making our nightly HIT (Hore Inspection Tour),
watching the black inside and out, digging night sights,
soul sounds and getting tight.

The grunts in the corner raise undisturbed hell
as the timid MP's freckles pale.
He walks past the dude high in the doorway,
in his lavender jump suit, to ask the mamma-san,
quietly, about curfew.

He chokes on the weed smoke as
he sees nothing his color here and
he fingers his army rosary—his .45.

But this is not Cleveland or Chicago;
he makes no one here cringe and
our gazes, like punji stakes, impale him.

We have all killed something recently,
know who owns the night,
and carry darkness with us.

WORDS

David Huddle

What did those girls say when you walked the strip
of tin shack bars, gewgaw stores, barbershops,
laundries and restaurants, most all of which
had beds in back, those girls who had to get up
in Saigon before dawn to catch their rides to Cu Chi,
packed ten to a Lambretta, chattering, happy
in their own lovely tongue, on the dusty
circus road to work, but then what did they say?

Come here, talk to me, you handsom, GI,
I miss you, I love you too much, you want
short time, go in back, I don't care, I want
your baby, sorry about that, GI,
you number ten. A history away
I translate dumbly what those girls would say.

TEMPLE AT QUAN LOI, 1969

Kevin Bowen

Outside the gate
the old woman
walks up the hill
from the temple.
Her pace
deliberate as a procession.
From the corner of an eye
she stares.
She must wish our deaths.
Beneath the white silk band
breasts ache for a husband.
She passes in mourning,
counting each step.
Her prayers rain down like rockets.

MEETING

Unknown North Vietnamese Soldier
Translated by Thanh T. Nguyen and Bruce Weigl

Last night, walking behind my unit under golden moonlight,
My rifle slung on my shoulder,
I met a peasant girl in Van.
Carrying two baskets of rice for the soldiers,
She crossed the bridge.

We met by chance
So I asked myself if such a love
Could ever be.
Shyly, she looked up at me.
Her dimpled cheeks made me love her, secretly.
Perhaps we would meet again.

BAMBOO BRIDGE

Doug Anderson

We cross the bridge, quietly.
The bathing girl does not see us
till we've stopped and gaped like fools.
There are no catcalls, whoops,
none of the things that soldiers do;
the most stupid of us is silent, rapt.
She might be fourteen or twenty,
sunk thigh deep in green water,
her woman's pelt a glistening corkscrew,
a wonder, a wonder she is: I forgot.
For a moment we all hold the same thought,
that there is life in life and war is shit.
For a song we'd all go to the mountains,
eat pineapples, drink goat's milk,
find a girl like this, who cares
her teeth are stained with betel nut,
her hands as hard as feet.
If I can live another month it's over,
and so we think a single thought,
a bell's resonance.

And then she turns and sees us there,
sinks in the water, eyes full of hate;
the trance broken.
We move into the village on the other side.

ON THE HIGHWAY

Nguyen Quang Thieu
Translated by the author and Martha Collins

Women carrying bamboo shrimp pots
Walk in a line on the side of the highway,
Dressed in brown and black.
Their hands, their feet, and their eyes show,
But they are brown and black too.

The pots on their shoulders are crescent moons pulled from
        mud,
The baskets at their hips are shaved heads that sway as they
        march.
Their shadows spill onto the highway in black puddles.

They walk like defeated soldiers, in silence;
The pot handles bend down, like empty rifles.
Their torn clothes, smelling of dried mud,
Are flags from village festivals that have ended.
Fish scales cling to their clothes and glitter like medals.
They expect no welcome, await no acclamation.

Like clouds floating heavy before a storm,
The women walk in a line on the side of the highway.
Where do they come from and where will they go,
Spreading the smell of crabs and snails around them?

WOMEN OF THE SOUTH

Luu Trong Lu
Translated by Don Luce, John Schafer, and Jacqui Chagnon

Tran thi Ly

Long hair, hair of a young mother,
Washed in the water of Thu Bon,
Adorning your body, wounded in a hundred places.
In life and death, always loyal.

Muoi Dong Tháp

Just turned twenty,
Leader of three hundred struggles.
One leg left, you stand erect,
A beautiful flag wrapping your body!

Nguyen thi Út

A guerrilla of the Delta
Carrying your only child on your hip,
Combing the river bank,
Striking the enemy as naturally as you go to market!

Ta thi Kieu

With a beautiful name from ancient times,
You're a faithful niece of Uncle Ho.
Striking the enemy, you're as a tiger.
Speaking of it, you smile like a flower.

Nguyen thi Dinh

In the assault you command a hundred squads.
Night returns, you sit mending fighters' clothes.
Woman general of the South, descended from Trac and Nhi,*
You've shaken the brass and steel of the White House.

*Trung Trac and Trung Nhi, the famous Trung sisters who led the Vietnamese against the Chinese about A.D. 40.

—1966

WORDS OF COMFORT

Do Tan
Translated by Huynh Sanh Thong

I want to mourn the stream,
I want to mourn the road,
I want to call the sun—
they all break down and weep.

Now weep no more, O river of farewells.
Now weep no more, O road of sad goodbyes.
Now weep no more, O hungry, tattered sun.
I'm nothing—don't blame me.

I'm just an orphan left distraught.
I'm just a lover, sorrow-crazed.
I'm just a widow numb with pain.
I'm nothing in the world today.

XIN LOI*

Doug Anderson

The man and woman, Vietnamese,
come up the hill,
carry something slung between them on a bamboo mat,
unroll it at my feet:
the child, iron gray, long dead,
flies have made him home.
His wounds are from artillery shrapnel.
The man and the woman look as if they are cast
from the same iron as their dead son,
so rooted are they in the mud.
There is nothing to say,
nothing in my medical bag, nothing in my mind.
A monsoon cloud hangs above,
its belly torn open on a mountain.

*Xin Loi (pronounced "sin loy") means "I am sorry" in Vietnamese.

It's Too Late

Jim Nye

The dumpy, toothless woman
   Mouth and gums red from betel nut
Screamed and cried
   Kneeling over the body
The kid got caught in a cross fire
   Spun around and dropped
Other villagers joined the keening
   And the wailing
And I thought,
   Lady, it won't help
   It won't bring him back
   If I thought it would
   I would kneel beside you
   And weep
But it's too late
There is nothing in this world
   As dead as a dead child.

The New Lullaby

Tran Da Tu
   Translated by Huynh Sanh Thong

Sleep well, my child—a shadow, not mama,
will tuck you snug in bed and help you sleep.
A tombstone is your pillow—let the sky
spread over you a blanket, keep you warm.
To shield you as a curtain, there's the rain.
A tree will be your fan, its leaves your roof.
The stars will twinkle as your mother's eyes.
The battlefield will be your romping ground.
Sleep well and smile, with blood upon your lips.
Bullets and bombs will sing your lullaby.

A Special Train

Daniel Hoffman

Banners! Bunting! The engine throbs
In waves of heat, a stifling glare
Tinges the observation car

And there, leaning over the railing,
What am I
Doing in the Orient?

Blackflies, shrapnel-thick, make bullocks
Twitch. The peasants stand
Still as shrines,

And look, in this paddy
A little boy is putting in the shoots.
He's naked in the sunlight. It's my son!

There he is again, in that
Field where the earth-walls meet.
It's his playtime. See, his hands are smeared

With mud, and now his white
Back is flecked with ash, is seared
By embers dropping from the sky—

The train chuffs past. I cry
Stop! Stop! We cross another paddy,
He's there, he's fallen in the mud, he moans my name.

In His Father's Footsteps

David Connolly

Having slapped a machete,
then a rock, from his hand,
I pushed the young boy
at gunpoint
toward the other villagers,
away from the still form
of his father.

Words were the only weapons
he had left.
"Someday, GI, mebbe *you* die!"

The B-40 shrapnel,
that weeks later
tore into me,
hit no harder.

Kids

Mark Kessinger

Kids were useful in Nam.
Every time they hit a village
they would bring out the candy
and food. Some hadn't eaten in days.
None had ever eaten candy.
First aid was routine. No questions
asked. Anyone who needed help got it.
The kids were grateful.
The villagers were grateful.
Sometimes they would fill sandbags
for the G.I.s, hoping they would
stay if they were fortified.
The kids would always let them know
where the pungi sticks were
as the joes patched them up.
American medicine was stronger
than the feces-coated sticks.

With G.I.s around, you were safe
from infection and the runs.
The country had never known Kaopectate.
Sometimes the kids would yank at
the sleeves of a soldier and
point out a man stepping off distances
and say "VEECEE. VEECEE."
The measurements were used to
direct fire into the camps

SECOND LIEUTENANT PARVIN ZELMER, U.S.M.C.

Bryan Alec Floyd

The reason he died?
He and the platoon came upon
three Vietnamese children, ages three, five, and eight,
who were playing with some tied-together pieces
of nice, shiny plastic that they had found in the grass.
The Lieutenant stood still
but ordered the rest of the platoon to fall back.
Then he asked the kids to put their toy,
a double booby trap, down gently,
but they did not understand
and pitched it to him,
and it bounced once and went boom,
gutting all four of them to shredded death.
A Congressman, upon hearing of the incident
from a news reporter,
asked the reporter one question:
"Was the booby trap theirs or ours?"
And his question was the answer.

Orphanage

Wendy Wilder Larsen

When I visited the orphanage
I went with balloons, hard candies
old *National Geographics.*

The children grabbed for everything.
I gave one a candy, others screamed
until seven or eight were clawing at my legs.

They popped the balloons
choked on the candies
shredded the magazines.

I looked over to the nun for help.

She stopped ladling gruel into the communal trough
put down the long tin spoon
and came across the room to tell me,

"Next time, if you come,
bring enough for everyone, or bring nothing."

I Met You in the Orphanage Yard

Thich Nhat Hanh

Your sad eyes
overflowed
with loneliness and pain.
You saw me.
You turned your face away.
Your hands drew circles
in the dusty ground.

I dared not ask you
where your father or mother was.
I dared not open up your wounds.
I only wished to sit with you a moment
and say a word or two.
O you small ones
of four or five—

your life buds already cut off,
already engulfed
by cruelty, hatred, and violence.

Why? Why?
My generation,
my cowardly age,
must shoulder the blame.

I'll go in a moment,
and you will remain
in the shabby yard.
Your eyes will return
to your familiar yard
and your fingers will draw again
those small circles
of pain
in the dusty ground.

A Letter to My Future Child

Tran Duc Uyen

Translated by Huynh Sanh Thong

When, dragging hideous crutches, war
is harrowing your land
and tearing up your country like a rag,
when paddy fields lack days to sprout young shoots
and there's no time for grass to grow,
I'm writing you this letter now
while I've no family yet.
Who will she be, your mother? I don't know.
But I believe you'll come into our world.
You'll enter it not while the curfew's on,
not stillborn and not writhing in an ambulance
like the second child of Aunt and Uncle Vinh,
or like many other children in these times.
Your father hopes you'll come into our world
with robust body and stout limbs.
You'll enter like a rising sun,
the Eastern sun, the summer sun.
You shall grow up amid the sounds of joy.

Along with vast green fields of rice,
along with grass and trees you'll live.
Hearing no plane by day, no gun at night,
you'll sleep untroubled sleep—
the sleep of radiant innocence.
Each morning, leaving home, I shall kiss you
beside the cradle fragrant with your mother's milk.
On your red lips shall bloom a smile,
a wholesome smile.
The greatest dreams on earth
I trust to you, my child.
You are the seed of humankind,
the hope, the future of the world.

At the Crossroads

Gerald McCarthy

This is where the children fell.
See how the dust absorbs them,
how the flies rise in slow circle
tracing the outline of their lives.

This is where the mother
kneeling in the scrub grass,
pressed her palms to the earth.

Listen, you can still hear her sigh.
Not the sound of the wind
although the wind carries it.
Not the noise of a train passing
in the late afternoon sun
although the train echoes it.

Her cries keep coming back;
across the field, lingering
in the withered leaves, the dry,
forgotten places.

CHILD OF MY LAI

Le Dan

Translated by Don Luce, John Schafer, and Jacqui Chagnon

Dear My Lai, my heart aches
With the cry of my young brother
Dying beside the corpses of his mother and grandmother,
Amid the sound of guns
And barbarous laughter.

Rice fields raise our children,
Why kill them, our people,
In so many places, so many times?
Why add hatred and violence?
Is it to achieve your rule
Upon this country
Of red blood and yellow skin?
Look at the heap of flesh and bones!
From thousands of years of struggle,
Each priceless person
Belongs to Viet Nam.
My young brother is like a bud
Growing on the tree of our nation.
The root, his father, he has never met;
The sap, his mother, he has never known,
And so it is with millions of brothers and sisters.
They have killed him, the bud of our tree;
They have killed his mother,
Killed his source of milk,
Yet can they kill his father
Who carries his gun against the invaders?
And can they kill the hatred
Within him as he dies?
His farewell is not his last word
For his brothers will be born and will grow,
Like the warriors of Phu Dong,
To repay the nation
Which has raised them,
The nation standing like a centennial tree.

And on its branches like the green buds
They will grow up,
Millions of hands to end this war
And drive from our country
These killers who cannot hide themselves.

Humanity will judge them
My Lai, I ache every second,
I cannot wait an hour
Or for evening to pass.
I must act now
To save old mothers
And young children.

FROM MY LAI THE THUNDER WENT WEST

Richard Ryan

and it all died down
to an underground
tapping and then that,
too, stopped dead.

In cornfield, wheat
field, a black
sheet of earth
was drawn neatly

across the seed
they planted.
And the fields turn
daily to the sun.

Come high Summer
and the first shoots
will appear, puzzling
the sun as, growing

through earth, growing
through grass, the
human crop they have sown—
child bone, wife

bone, man
bone will stand
wavering in the pale fields:
the silent, eye-

less army will
march west through
Autumn and Europe
until, streaked

with December rain
they will stand in
New York and Texas;
as the lights click

out across America
they will fence in
the houses, tapping
on window, tapping

on door. Till
dawn, then rain only:
from sea to sea drifting,
drops of bright ruby.

THE TRIAL

Lowell Jaeger

First I wasted feathered things
with the long gun my uncle handed me
down. No, first I pulled the trigger
in my mind. I flew a coon's tail
on a leather thong as I pedaled
up and down the pavement of my primitive
town. I stomped on a green snake's head.
Imagine the magic rush of cool steel,
to splinter pine planks at fifty yards.
Then bored with targets bleeding sap,
I dropped a goldfinch from his perch.
I was the perfect priest of make-believe.
Holding him weightless in my rawhide glove,
I rubbed his colors on my sleeve.

Q. *One burst or semi-automatic?*
        A. *Semi-automatic, Sir.*
Q. *Who did you fire at?*
        A. *Into the ditch, Sir.*
Q. *What at in the ditch?*
        A. *At the people in the ditch, Sir.*

With a driver's license I felt bad
laughing with chums on our way to school,
thumping twice over anything that moved.
I learned how never to use the rearview
mirror, how days were fresh concrete
slates I had to hurry down
from one duty to the next. Nights we patrolled
county trunks, our searchlights reaching
into poplars and pines for dark eyes
staring out from inside some other world.
I squeezed an open beer between my legs.
I had to play the radio loud, close my eyes
the second before . . . so I couldn't hear them
drop in the ditch, couldn't see their surprise.

Q. You don't recall how many?
> *A. No, Sir. It wasn't significant to me at the time, Sir.*
Q. Do you recall the sex of these people?
> *A. No, Sir, I don't.*
Q. Were there any children?
> *A. Yes, Sir, I believe there were, Sir.*

The uniform fit. My father and his father
each had forgotten their war. I mailed snapshots
home: me with all my brass buttons
saluting the flag; me at parade rest, shot
against an enameled backdrop projecting
a halo around my ears. Combat fatigues
clung like reptile skins as we hacked
through steamy green. Insects, vicious
as piranhas, jumped on my neck. Bloated
snakes, bright as Cadillacs, dared me
to pass. Monsoon fungi peeled my flesh
back to shins of red scales, tender bone.
Picture me reaching under the sharp leaves, shaking
vines. Spiders! Spiders! The enemy had guns of their own.

Q. How far were you from them when you fired?
> *A. The muzzle would have been five feet, Sir.*
Q. Didn't you say yesterday that they were apparently all dead?
> *A. I said they were apparently all dead, Sir. But I don't know exactly if they were dead, Sir.*
Q. Why were they apparently dead?
> *A. They were lying in the ditch and weren't moving.*

Mushroom creatures, hoodoo gnomes of rice
and bamboo. Rats! Brown rats in tribes. . . .
Uncle Wayne said with the cylinders honed
she'd turn over and fire, even in the weeds
up to her door handles and the bed loaded
with old water coolers and box springs.
My last furlough I hiked through cow chips
to turn the key. Rats! Tribes of whiskers
and wet feet scuffed over my shoulders and down

my sleeve. I beat them and beat them till I hung
onto the wheel and screamed. With an M-16
I broke their little stick bodies in that ditch. . . .
Cry for us all, for learning our lessons well.
Sentence me where you will; I've been to hell.

A POISON TREE

Elliot Richman

Seven guys from the 7th CAV,
2 white, 5 black.
Hands tied. Feet tied.
All blood. All butchered.
Blossom
apple bright
upside down
from that tree
33 klicks west
of My Lai

7

A Dark Tolling

CHRISTMAS EVE 1972

Don Luce

It's
  Been
    a
      Bleak
        December

With
  Nixon's
    B-52
      Bombers
        Bringing

Messages
  of
      Peace
      Peace
      Peace
      Peace
      Peace
and Hanoi goes up in flames
and I wonder what has happened
to my friends there.

Two Villages

Grace Paley

In Duc Ninh a village of 1,654 households
Over 100 tons of rice and cassava were burned
18,138 cubic meters of dike were destroyed
There were 1077 air attacks
There is a bomb crater that measures 150 feet across
It is 50 feet deep

Mr. Tat said: The land is more exhausted than the people
                I mean to say that the poor earth
                is tossed about
                thrown into the air again and again
                it knows no rest

                whereas the people have dug tunnels
                and trenches they are able in this way
                sto lead normal family lives

  In Trung Trach
a village of 850 households
a chart is hung in the House of Tradition

rockets	522
attacks	1201
big bombs	6998
napalm	1383
time bombs	267
shells	12291
pellet bombs	2213

Mr. Tuong of the Fatherland Front
has a little book
in it he keeps the facts
carefully added

Corporal Charles Chungtu, U.S.M.C.

Bryan Alec Floyd

This is what the war ended up being about:
we would find a V.C. village,
and if we could not capture it
or clear it of Cong,
we called for jets.
The jets would come in, low and terrible,
sweeping down, and screaming,
in their first pass over the village.
Then they would return, dropping their first bombs
that flattened the huts to rubble and debris.
And then the jets would sweep back again
and drop more bombs
that blew the rubble and debris
to dust and ashes.
And then the jets would come back once again,
in a last pass, this time to drop napalm
that burned the dust and ashes to just nothing.
Then the village
that was not a village anymore
was our village.

Mission

L. Dean Minze

Ninety-nine gone,
One more to go.
Nerve endings screaming,
Screaming,
Screaming turbines,
Gauges aquiver,
Roll out, run up,
Brakes release,
Release,
Release from fear
And pain
And all but
Mission.

Untitled
Robert Lax

look
where
Christ's
blood

streams

in
the
fir-
ma
ment

look
where
your

broth-
er

is

splash-
'd

a-
gainst

the

sky

PETE

Sharon Fuhrman

He was a fighter pilot first
A husband second
A father third.
We loved each other dearly,
But I know he was never really mine.
He belonged to the sky
And now the sky has claimed him.

DIARY OF A MAC* HOUSEWIFE

Linda Williamson

Your first morning out, I washed the sheets,
Made neat rows in the cupboards, and paid the bills

On the second day, I went to lunch.
Walked the stores awhile, bought you some sox.

I wrote your mother on the third day,
Sent pictures of our son. He has your eyes.

I pressed your uniform, it smelled of shaving lotion.
I turned around, the kitchen was empty.

It rained one day, and I tried to read.
Without thinking, I set your place at the table.

On the sixth day, the telephone didn't ring.
Each of the airplanes wasn't you.

Tonight I watch the moon on your child's face.
The hope of headlights brings me nothing.

*Military Airlift Command

No Complaints

L. L. Case

According to columnists Rowland Evans and Robert Novak (October 11th), it seems that "a special task force studying the psychological reaction in the villages indicate no mass anti-U.S. feeling resulting from the bombings." And "the counter-insurgency mission . . . that has gone into the villages to win over the people has not sent back a single complaint about the bombing."

We have just received the results of the latest South Vietnam Government Public Opinion Agency Poll, which should take care of the cynics among us. The questions asked by their interviewers were these:

Do you have any complaints about the way American planes bombed your village?	Yes	0%
	No	24%
	No opinion	76%
Which do you prefer: bombing, burning, or machine-gunning?	Bombing	20%
	Burning	2%
	Machine-gunning	2%
	No opinion	76%
Are you satisfied with the way the bombing has been handled, or shall we shoot you now?	Satisfied	24%
	Shoot now	0%
	No opinion	76%

The rather high no-opinion vote was because of death, etc.

Driving Through Minnesota During the Hanoi Bombings

Robert Bly

We drive between lakes just turning green;
Late June. The white turkeys have been moved
A second time to new grass.
How long the seconds are in great pain!
Terror just before death,
Shoulders torn, shot
From helicopters. "I saw the boy
being tortured with a telephone generator,"
The sergeant said.
"I felt sorry for him
And blew his head off with a shotgun."
These instants become crystals,
Particles
The grass cannot dissolve. Our own gaiety
Will end up
In Asia, and you will look down in your cup
And see
Black Starfighters.
Our own cities were the ones we wanted to bomb!
Therefore we will have to
Go far away
To atone
For the suffering of the stringy-chested
And the short rice-fed ones, quivering
In the helicopter like wild animals,
Shot in the chest, taken back to be questioned.

Lines Written on the Occasion of President Nixon's Address to the Nation, May 8, 1972

A. J. M. Smith

"The man with the acid face
Under the hammer of glass
Imperils the pure place."
Thirty-six years ago
The muse of political verse,
By the time's distempers crazed,
Brought these prophetic lines
Into a poet's mind—
Apposite then
And now, godammit, again.

The man in the box of glass
Speaks to a million rooms
With a sharp, determined face
And an obstinate, truculent voice.
He speaks of enlarging the war
To hasten the coming of peace;
Of care for the "boys" he leaves
To suffer for him and for us;
And, wickedest folly, of honor,
Not knowing it long ago lost.

The irresponsible bombs
Dropped by anonymous hands
Into invisible clouds
Splash into fire and blood
On military targets alone,
Including alas!—O crocodile tears!—
Mother and baby, ox and old man
—Not white or American though,
Yet inescapable parts
Of the Chiefs of Staff's overall plan.

The man with the acid mind
Speaks from the box of glass.
We listen in darkening rooms.
But not only America listens;

The Tartar and Muscovite hear.
We have made of the symbol of love
The defoliate rose.
Must we foresee our New York,
As Gray foresaw London,
"Purg'd by the sword/And beautifyed by fire"?

SCATTERING FLOWERS

George Hitchcock

> "It is our best and prayerful judgment that they
> [air attacks on North Vietnam] are a necessary part
> of the surest road to peace."
>
> —Lyndon B. Johnson

There is a dark tolling in the air,
an unbearable needle in the vein,
the horizon flaked with feathers of rust.
From the caves of drugged flowers
fireflies rise through the night:
they bear the sweet gospel of napalm.

Democracies of flame are declared
in the villages, the rice fields
seethe with blistered reeds.
Children stand somnolent in their crutches.
Freedom, a dancing-girl,
lifts her petticoats of gasoline,
and on the hot sands of a deserted beach
a wild horse struggles, choking
in the noose of diplomacy.

Now in their cane chairs the old men
who listen for the bitter wind
of bullets, spread on their thighs
maps, portfolios, legends of hair,
and photographs of dark Asian youths
who are already dissolving into broken water.

BALLET

Milton Kaplan

After reading the latest
peace proposal
in the paper, last night
I went to the Met
to see Nureyev dance
and there was one moment
in "Swan Lake"
when he leaped high
in the luminous air
and for a split second
just hung weightless
not like a bird
but like a man
who had somehow
learned to spurn
the laws that drag
him down to earth
and for an instant
I really believed
it might all
be possible.

The Fall of Da Nang

Gerald McCarthy

Tonight the newspapers report
the air-lift evacuation of Da Nang has failed;
that South Vietnamese soldiers shot their way
through crowds of civilians
to board the last plane that landed.

Years have passed since Aubrey and I
got high together, watching the night sky
across the South China Sea.
Near Monkey Mountain the Viet Cong are entrenched
hitting the airfield with artillery fire.

I think back to an evening in July
in that same city, when I waited for a plane
to get me out.
My friends watch television.

*   *   *

I pry open the window, listen to the noise
of a passing car on the wet road.
The news interrupts a commercial
with a special bulletin. I watch the faces
of Vietnamese children: the same tired faces
that will always be there.

My friends leave to play poker:
nickel, dime, quarter, they say.
I smoke cigarettes, drink beer.
It's Saturday night, the end of March.

After the Fall of Saigon

Walter McDonald

A mad man aging hard can't fight a war
forever. Think pity and the mind turns cold.
He still sees children and old men

ragged and golden, crawling the base dump
for scraps of food at sundown.
Years after Saigon, he's like a wall:

lets no one know him, but his name.
Stone-faced, he tries to wish it all away,
a harmless Buddha with a green patina,

envies the lucky ones who didn't go.
Even good booze can't burn the fungus out,
down where it doesn't show,

the mind's own groin. He takes another shot
to hold him till it's dark, but after that,
they're back.

Freedom Bird

Jon Forrest Glade

I left Vietnam aboard a hospital plane,
with no windows for patients,
so I didn't see the take-off.
I remember everybody was nervous
as we turned and taxied,
afraid we might catch a rocket
or one last mortar round.
Everyone held their breath
as the plane gathered speed.
When we felt the wheels
leave the ground,
someone yelled out,
"Good-bye, you rotten nasty motherfucker."

I wish I had left Vietnam
aboard a real Freedom Bird

with stewardesses and a view;
but, the way I left wasn't bad.
I laughed half way to Japan.

APRIL 30, 1975
John Balaban

for Bui Ngoc Huong

The evening Nixon called his last troops off,
the church bells tolled across our states.
We leaned on farmhouse porch pilings, our eyes
wandering the lightning bug meadow thick with mist,
and counted tinny peals clanking out
through oaks around the church belltower,
You asked, "Is it peace, or only a bell ringing?"

This night the war has finally ended.
My wife and I sit on a littered park bench
sorting out our shared and separate lives
in the dark, in silence, before a quiet pond
where ducks tug slimy papers and bits of soggy bread.
City lights have reddened the bellies of fumed clouds
like trip flares scorching skies over a city at war.

In whooshing traffic at the park's lit edge,
red brake lights streak to sudden halts:
a ski-masked man staggers through lanes,
maced by a girl he tried to mug.
As he crashes to curb under mercury lamps,
a man snakes towards him, wetting his lips,
twirling the root of his tongue like a dial.

Some kids have burnt a bum on Brooklyn Bridge.
Screaming out of sleep, he flares the causeway.
The war returns like figures in a dream.
In Vietnam, pagodas chime their bells.
"A Clear Mind spreads like the wind.
By the Lo waterfalls, free and high,
you wash away the dust of life."

CAPTAIN MAINERO

Peter Ulisse

NVA tanks burst through gates
of the Presidential Palace.
Thousands of South Vietnamese
storm our position.
They know what comes next,
would sell their own brothers
for a seat on a chopper.
From telephone poles to walls
to concertina wire above
they hurl themselves toward us.
We tear-gas the stairwells,
club them with rifles,
but we can't stop the wave
as ARVNs leave families,
tear off their uniforms
to merge with the crowd.

We marines hold our ground,
then board the last chopper
as mothers throw babies
hoping we catch one,
teenagers cling
to landing gear below,
fall like rocks
when we don't take them in.

I think of ten years,
fifty thousand lives,
wonder why we can't
at least like the French,
march off with honor.

As Those Americans Flee

Nguyen Chi Thien
Translated by Huynh Sanh Thong

As those Americans flee and leave the South,
the earth's most powerful country groans with shame.
In spite of prison, sickness, hunger, cold,
the muse keeps shooting, bullets still galore,
because she knows a morrow, far but bright,
shall not belong to evil force.
despair spreads everywhere,
hope is but destroyed,
the people wail and weep the long, long night—
yet, lying fettered on the ground, the muse
still sings in silence, bruised but game,
making the heart a magic looking-glass
in which the Communists show their true shape.
All must decay—but poetry shall endure
to vanquish space, to triumph over time,
while in due course all enemy steel will rust.

1975

FLYING BLIND
Trinh T. Minh-Ha

                    bodies
against empty bodies
canned and lifted in the air
you flew away all lights off
in fear of shots from below
you flew blind and fragile
knowing not when or where
nor how far off before
they hit your brittle wings
you flew away from home
from the place you once were
the same sky you gazed at
under your homely screen
you flew away from fire
from death in between cries
or lives in between debts
for bullets don't have eyes
and no matter how fast
how far you flee you know
firing away remains
the aim of those who stay

PACKING
Tran Thi Nga

I packed strange things
sandalwood soap from Hong Kong,
12 of my best ao dai,
my collection of tiny perfume bottles.

We all wanted to bring our mothers.
None of us could.
We had so many false starts
I never said goodbye to her.

One morning I made an incense offering
on my father's altar.

"You going today?" Mother asked.
"No," I said. "I just missed him
dreamt about him
wanted him to wish us luck."

I left my mother in our house on the street
that had been named General de Gaulle,
then Cong Ly, or Justice Street,
and then Cach Mang, Revolution Street.

I left my money on the outside porch
and never saw her again.

The Airport

Tran Thi Nga

In the yard outside the hangar
were hundreds of Vietnamese
lying on their mats with their luggage
and their children all around them.
We were worried about the crowds,
about being searched,
about the gold and dollars on our persons,
about what we would say if we were caught.
We walked to the snack bar for dinner
and paid 19,000 piasters for noodles.
When we got back, it was dark.
Our spot was crowded with people,
embassy people, MACV people.
My son thought he recognized a secret agent
and hid his face.
Men with walkie-talkies were everywhere.

When an official Vietnamese asked us
to leave our place,
I pleaded with an American Lt.-Colonel
who allowed us to stay.
We had a tiny baby with us, my granddaughter.
I told him we had missed our charter
and wanted to go as soon as possible.
He said the sooner the better.
I said the office could not blame us
if we did not take the plane they had chartered.
He said to stay together
and go to the Philippines, not to Guam.
I said, anywhere but Vietnam.

ESCAPE

Tran Thi Nga

We made lists.
That was the manifest,
name, sex, age.
When the captain came for us,
we went quickly to the bus,
squeezed into the front
with all our luggage on one seat
as he had told us to.
A man asked who could speak English.
I was quiet.
It was dark.
He told us to be silent
or we would be shot.
We held our breath.
There wasn't a sound on that crowded bus.

As we approached, the plane made a huge noise,
like a C-130.
It opened at the back, a mouth.
We were thrown in like packets.
The pilot ordered *stop*
just as the last of our group was in.
Hundreds of us sat on the floor,
a huge string tied around us,
our babies on our laps.
Many were sick.

We arrived at Clark Field, Philippines, at 1:30 A.M.
Everyone was quiet.
We were handed medicine, blankets, mattresses.
People were everywhere.
There was much red tape,
name, sex, age.

I heard over the radio
soon after we left, the Vietnamese MPs,
not wanting any more people to leave the country,
arrested everyone at the airport.

8

All Your World of Griefs

The Sea, the World, and the Boat People
Ha Huyen Chi

Those boats keep rushing out to restless sea
with wind-puffed sails and souls stretched taut and tense.
In quest of hope they will go courting death,
dreaming that one day freedom shall be theirs.

Those boats keep riding over turbulent waves,
defying every peril on the way.
They'd rather leave their bones inside a shark
than rot as slaves inside a tyrant's jail.

Boat people wave to ships that will not stop—
each second of their time means life or death.
Voices grow hoarse appealing to men's hearts,
and bitter tears well up in hollow eyes.

Small children's corpses sink to ocean depths.
Young girls' pure, virgin bodies are defiled.
People in death cannot stay whole, unmaimed.
And drunk on blood's foul smell, the pirates laugh.

Those boats keep heading one by one toward death.
Men turn their backs and hide their cowardice.
Where has it fled, the conscience of mankind?
The world just opens wide its eyes and stares.

O ports and harbors where those boats may drift—
open your hearts and let them come inside.
Give those who've lost their country, lost their all,
a chance to live out their expatriate lives.

The Boat People
Thich Nhat Hanh

You stay up late tonight, my brothers.
This I know,
because the boat people
on the high seas
never dare to sleep.

I hear the cry of the winds
around me—
total darkness.

Yesterday they threw the dead bodies
of their babies and children
into the water.
Their tears once again filled
the ocean of suffering.
In what direction are their boats drifting
at this moment?

You stay up late tonight, brothers,
because the boat people
on the high seas
are not certain at all that humankind exists.
Their loneliness
is so immense.

The darkness has become one with the ocean;
and the ocean, an immense desert.

You stay up all night, brothers,
and the whole universe
clings to your being awake.

REFUGEE

Trinh T. Minh-Ha

just imagine yourself in a position
where you feel acutely responsible
for the one decisive turn of history
yours in the world's perfect circle
where you know precisely each decision
each single move you undertake
reverberates upon thousands
thousand lives with you
you despite yourself choose
reaching out to countless faces
haunted in your dreams
dwelling inside your meager self

imagine these endless constraints
of power you share your life with
every minute moment you lead
imagine one simple morning one night
who knew whether it was day or night
for reasons beyond you
beyond every yes or no you could say
you ran straight ahead
to the night of your soul
the night of your soulless being
that very night the endless unnamed reigned
you ran and since then run naked
empty hand empty mind leaving
your land your home your belongings
your beloved dead and living
the only self you cared for behind
who knew what else you let run
and forgot to ever name
you yours your own humaneness
you ran mute forlorn
among thousands blind to thousands
crushed yet touchless in lonely sphere
echoes of your steps your heartbeat drowned
stifling in the thick of empty sights
you were there and one
among the packed breathless silent crowd
so dense they said you could walk on it
on thousand voiceless presences
verging to the frontier of pure absence
neither there nor anywhere else
facing the threshold of nothingness
you stood speechless living no thing aloud
your heart coming to a halt barely halt
hollowing out the being of your most
utmost inner void

A New Year's Wish for a Little Refugee

Tran Mong Tu

Let me send you some words, a simple wish.
It's New Year's Eve—black night shrouds skies and seas.
A miracle saved your life, O little child!
Aboard that boat, all perished, all but you.

Let me send you some words, a simple wish.
New Year's should be a day for love and joy.
But where are both your parents, little child?
You're pouring tears, enough to fill the sea.

Let me send you some words, a simple wish.
This New Year's Day, alone on foreign soil,
you'll feel just like a seaweed washed ashore—
you won't know what the future holds for you.

No lack of kindly hands that will grab you
and take you home to change what's now your name.
They'll turn you into some new human breed
that thinks your yellow skin is cause for shame.

They will send you to school where you'll be taught
their land's own history, modern ways of life.
You will grow up denying what you are—
you'll never hear your forebears spoken of.

Let me send you some words, a simple wish
for this new year, for scores of years to come.
O little child, may you keep it intact,
your past of sorrows, all your world of griefs.

New Year's Eve, 1980

Deep as the Sea
Lamont Steptoe

War
has wounded me
invisible wound
deep as the sea
invisible wound
deep as the sea

Untitled
Dick Shea

i feel nothing on being back
just the feeling of wanting to be somewhere else
not back there
or here

just somewhere else

COMING HOME
W. D. Ehrhart

San Francisco airport—

no more corpsmen stuffing ruptured chests
with cotton balls and not enough heat tabs
to eat a decent meal.

I asked some girl to sit
and have a Coke with me.
She thought I was crazy;
I thought she was going to call a cop.

I bought a ticket for Philadelphia.
At the loading gate, they told me:
"Thank you for flying TWA;
we hope you will enjoy your flight."

No brass bands;
no flags,
no girls,
no cameramen.

Only a small boy who asked me
what the ribbons on my jacket meant.

THE LONGEST WAR
Jan Barry

The longest war is over
Or so they say
Again
But I can still hear the gunfire
Every night
From
My bed.

The longest nightmare
Never seems to
Ever
Quite come
To
An end.

NIGHTMARE

Nguyen Quang Thieu
Translated by the author and Martha Collins

for John Baca, American Veteran of the Vietnam War

His dog licks and licks his chest.
Its tongue is a small flame
Bringing warmth, like steam from a stove.
The tenderness of the dog makes him weep.

At the start of his dream a gun fires;
At the end of his dream is the Mekong River
Where fishermen wind cloth
Around their heads and cast their nets.
The dusk lowers its yellow wings on the river.

The bullets are hairless sewer-rats
Rushing into palm-thatched huts,
Chewing the nets drying along the bank.

John Baca bursts out laughing
And squeezes the yellow-toothed rats.
Hairless, slick, they slide
Through his shaking fingers.
John Baca stops laughing.

John Baca squeezed the trigger
Of his gun twenty years ago
But the bullets still fly.

His dog licks and licks
And licks and licks.

From
"CLOSURE: A MUCH NEEDED WAR"

Steve Mason

Maybe we should back it up a bit . . .

Nobody ever
wanted to belong
like we did.
To belong to a thing so beautiful.
So right. So alive.
One, sweet breath after another,
being an American
was a lot like breathing.
How could you not?

Well, after Vietnam
many of us did try to hold our breath.
Fists jammed deep into our pockets,
we turned our collars up
and walked through marriages and jobs,
nightmares and daymares
clear across America.
Eyes on the curb of our sanity
we whistled the red, white and blues
like we were blown
through James Moody's flute
till there was no air left
(even to cry the blues).

As for me,
I darted across my reality
like somebody let loose
the pinched ends
of a too full balloon.
Whizzzzzzz!
And I bounced off the wall
useless and spent
into a leather crack
at the front edge of a donated Vet Center chair
(right next to you)

looking like I felt—
a limp dick.
(And as I recall, hah!
you didn't look so fuckin' great
yourself.)

So we sat there
(all across the country)
in small, unmerry little bands
looking, no doubt, from each ceiling
like a large, nervous smoke ring!
And proceeded to huff and puff
and talk our way
out of the jungle,
all the way home.
One day, each of our group leaders
will be bronzed
and appropriately awarded,
unto himself, a park.
Until then,
they'll have to be content
with merely having saved
a lot of lives.
My team leader was Bill Mahedy.
I would have been history
five years ago . . .
Oh, those group sessions!
   "Yeah, and my specialty
   was cuttin' ears off . . ."

   "Shit. I been married to more women
   than is in this room right now.
   I mean than there is guys
   in this room right now. Oh shit.
   You know what I mean . . ."

   "I don't trust anybody. Not anybody.
   Not even my kids. Not even the dog."

   "I'll give those muthas the benefit
   of my education. I'll go ninja

and blow up every V.A. building
in the country!"
Many cheers and catcalls
and a chorus of Fuckin A's!!!)
An' my group had a dumbass in it!
who would say things like,
    "Man is probably the only animal
    who takes prisoners.
    Certainly, he is the only one
    who denies whole portions
    of his population access
    to the general food supply . . ."
Boy, was I a dumbass
but everybody was nice to me
(I brought the doughnuts).
I maintained I had existential anxiety,
they maintained I was just a dumbass.
God, what perspective!
I loved those guys.
And I like to think
they loved me back.

When the group would break up
we'd take it outside to the fenders.
Sometimes until dawn.
The night air helped cool the rage.
We discussed how to make a difference.
At such times I could feel America
listening to our conversations
as she lay in bed. Thinking.

Well. America woke up.
And she continued to listen.
And finally she sat down
across the table from us
and she just called our hand.
I figure we're holding
aces over jacks—
truth over courage.
And if she agrees—

we've won the pot
and the deal.
And the deal is:
We're out of the box now.
Out of the closet.
We're standin' in the door
and "outside" we've got it to do.
Only our war is over.

America is waiting for us, now.
And the world is waiting for America.
It won't be enough to wear buttons.
It won't be enough to coach
a girls' softball team
when the children of other poor men
are too weak to stand.
It's our play now.
The truth of our perspective
must be assimilated
by our nation's system of values.
And added to the consciousness
of the world.
Until then, no closure.

WAITER IN A CALIFORNIA VIETNAM RESTAURANT

Clarence Major

With the smell of firebombing
still in his nose,
he brings our plates to the table
pausing for a vertiginous instant,
holding them like they are two stones.
When he tries to smile his face
        turns purple like sky above
that Red River delta.
He once stood against a tree
with both arms above his head,
like somebody about to dance
flamenco, but he wasn't, it was
the time of the spring offensive,
and he was looking into the barrel
of a rifle held by a boy
whose trigger-finger
        had turned to stone.

PEER GROUP

Bill Shields

me & the boys got the highest rate
of alcoholism & drug abuse & divorce
& mental illness & suicide
than any other group
in America
It's good to see us win
for a change

CURSE THE RAINBOW

Jacqueline M. Loring

As the sky brightens,
our children flee the porch.
Through the trees,
I follow their tumblesaulting, like monkeys in the pasture.
You remain behind the screen
in the mist that blurs your face, criss-crosses your eyes.
Your plea through the distant thunder
calls me back. I reach unfolding fingers
for you to follow, pause and breathe.
You move outside, small,
bare steps avoid the bounty of the rain.
Your pounding memory searches for running children,
darts among the branches, listens to the howling
wind.

As the clouds clear the sky from gray
to sunset scarlet, again, I wait
through the pounding, my back to the children
and the trees. I damn the storm, the barbed wire between us,
want to scrape napalm into your memory
to ease your pain and mine.
As one last lightning strikes, I wonder if I can go on.
I clearly see that neither your laughing children
nor my patient love can hold you
from this moment. Still, the sky clears,
our bed stays warm, our children grow,
fathered by that piece of you we own,
uncursed.

Song of Napalm
Bruce Weigl
for my wife

After the storm, after the rain stopped pounding,
We stood in the doorway watching horses
Walk off lazily across the pasture's hill.
We stared through the black screen,
Our vision altered by the distance
So I thought I saw a mist
Kicked up around their hooves when they faded
Like cut-out horses
Away from us.
The grass was never more blue in that light, more
Scarlet; beyond the pasture
Trees scraped their voices into the wind, branches
Criss-crossed the sky like barbed wire
But you said they were only branches.

Okay. The storm stopped pounding.
I am trying to say this straight: for once
I was sane enough to pause and breathe
Outside my wild plans and after the hard rain
I turned my back on the old curses. I believed
They swung finally away from me . . .

But still the branches are wire
And thunder is the pounding mortar,
Still I close my eyes and see the girl
Running from her village, napalm
Stuck to her dress like jelly,
Her hands reaching for the no one
Who waits in waves of heat before her.

So I can keep on living,
So I can stay here beside you,
I try to imagine she runs down the road and wings
Beat inside her until she rises
Above the stinking jungle and her pain
Eases, and your pain, and mine.

But the lie swings back again.
The lie works only as long as it takes to speak
And the girl runs only as far
As the napalm allows
Until her burning tendons and crackling
Muscles draw her up
Into that final position
Burning bodies so perfectly assume. Nothing
Can change that; she is burned behind my eyes
And not your good love and not the rain-swept air
And not the jungle green
Pasture unfolding before us can deny it.

LAST ASYLUM

Gary Rafferty

I haven't laughed this way
for a long time.

In the safety
of Ward 8
we are the child-warriors
who went to Nam.
Irreverent, outrageous
not yet butchered.

& Kelly, that crazy bastard,
makes us laugh
'till our sides ache.

The funniest part?
When Howard, our Korean Vet asks
in perfect innocence,

"Do you guys know how fast
a grass hut burns?"

We make zippo motions
with our hands
& tears roll down our cheeks.

"Do we know how fast
a grass hut burns?!"

Shit, Howard,
half of 'Nam
is STILL on fire
because of us!
& so are we.

*Ward 8: a psychiatric ward in a VA hospital.

NAM NIGHTMARES

Bill Shields

I lie here in my bed one more night
wanting a woman to hold
or a knife
& wonder
if
a man in Ho Chi Minh City
is also sweating thru the sheets

Twins

Gary Rafferty

Somewhere in Vietnam
my twin lives
by another restless river.
Oceans apart,
each built our homes alone.
Though the war was over
there's bunkers under both.
Our wives grew tired watching
us fight the war alone.
They left for men who had not fought.

Ghosts still inhabit our days
hover behind, faithful friends.
When we take boats out to fish
they sit beside, weightless as birds
careful not to scare the fish.
Yet, we worry
their weight will sink us.
Now & then,
if you stand on either shore
you'll hear us speak to them.

Our children can't understand.
Although poets
we're wordless to explain,
we stammer:
"I grew up on a different planet
than this one."
They think us mad.

In truceless nightmares
our hands find their way
around each other's throats.

Because we are brothers
there are tears in our eyes
when we wake.

In the Labor Market at Giang Vo

Pham Tien Duat

Translated by Nguyen Ba Chung and Kevin Bowen

I don't dare ask who you are,
selling your strength out on the street.
The rich need someone to put up their new houses.
They don't care who you are, where you come from.

I care. You are the dark alluvial soil
torn from the river bend, the jagged rock
wrenched from the mountain.
One difference though—hunger gnaws at your guts.

These days every village must be a great city,
stacks of food shimmer and dance in the street.
Not lack of work, but this new life gives birth to new lines of
    workers.
A new sky must mean new kinds of clouds.

Dusk crawls up the road. The crowd thins out.
No one left but you. I recognize you now,
the look of quiet tenacity, the scar,
the last broken shard of the war.

1993

OUTLIVING OUR GHOSTS

Doug Anderson

For Al Miller

You show me the X ray,
tell me how the bullet clipped the rim of your helmet,
sheared off the top of your ear,
continued downward into the shoulder
where the nerves cable under the collarbone,
soft as the white of an eye, and there,
broke up and stopped. The Jews say,
Bad times past are good to tell of.
Al, did we dream it all?
With your fingers you trace bullet fragments,
how they have moved over the years
as your body continued its path toward the death
that touched your shoulder twenty years ago
and spun you back into life with your eyes open.
Flesh alive then is no longer part of us.
If each cell is new every seven years,
what is the heart's tattoo?
And the years between. You finding Buddha
in a young Vietnamese you killed;
me getting sober, seeing my life stand up
as from the tall grass,
where it had lain all this time, covered with signs.
Talking again we honor the darkness,
breathe again the sweet air of a second life.
We are here and we are whole.
I hold the X ray up to the light:
the fragments still in your flesh,
bright winter stars.

Scars

Truong Tran

my father's body is a map
a record of his journey

he carries a bullet
lodged in his left thigh
there is a hollow where it entered
a protruding bump where it sleeps
the doctors say it will never awaken

it is the one souvenir he insists on keeping
mother has her own opinions
bô cua con díên—your father is crazy

as a child
I wanted a scar just like my father's
bold and appalling   a mushroom explosion
that said I too was at war
instead I settled for a grain of rice
a scar so small look closely there
here between the eyes
a bit to the right
there on the bridge of my nose

father says I was too young to remember
it happened while I was sleeping
leaking roof the pounding rain
drop after drop after drop

WIND AND WIDOW

Le Thi May
Translated by Nguyen Ba Chung

Wind widow willowy
off the arms of dawn and grass
full-chested breath
after so much lovemaking in the night

patches of cloud-clothes discarded in the air
lipstick
sunrise
facial cream
aroma moon of the fourteenth day

wind widow after each makeup
backward glances to another time of sadness and laughter

grass
and dawn rises trembling
separated from wind after lovemaking
all night
. . .
wind elegiac-wind
strands of hair from women who died in the bombing
strands of hair from widows who raised orphaned children
the war after ten years have passed—

Twenty Years

Do Tan

Translated by Nguyen Ngoc Bich, Burton Raffel, and W. S. Merwin

The girl grew up to become a woman
the boy grew up to become a man
man met woman in the forbidden wood
their child was the gift of spring.

The spring child joined the revolution
the revolution was a ravening cannibal
man's portion was exile, prison, bullets,
with sun, roses, and a blood-reeking flag.

The woman weeps for the girl that was
the man weeps for the boy that was
their child sleeps the eternal sleep in the earth
the spring hangs its head and sighs.

TRACKS OF MY TEARS

Bill Shields

it's a small trail of hydraulic fluid
she leaves behind her motorized
wheelchair moving
that tiny spina bifida
child between classes

                           this child

born twelve years after the last
55 gallon drum of Agent Orange
was spilled into the Mekong Delta
pays for her father's life
with her own
landing
zone

9

The Names Rise Up

ELEGY TO AN UNWEPT SOLDIER

Nguyen Quoc Vinh

You, like many heroes,
Have given up your life
To the call of the country.
But there are no laurels
For you, the unwept soldier.
In a struggle without glory.

All is lost
for nothing.
And so you lie here.
A disgrace.
Your sacrifice unsung.

The children.
Sheltered in schools
When you collapsed in battle,
Have never known of you.
They, like merry birds.
Sing, but not for you.
They offer you no flower.
They give you no hymn of praise.
They, who will one day
Join you in oblivion.

You have been but a shadow
Of a life too short,
Of a spring that never came.
And your story swirls
Like withered leaves
In the maelstrom.
The sky sours its peace,
Clouds blacken their faces,
The wind billows its rage
They, too, turn their back on you.

It is not your fault.
It is not their fault.
It is no one's fault.
It is everyone's fault.

You have no one's pity.

Tears have dried
From the wrinkled eyes
Of a heartbroken mother,
Who, like a marble statue
Hoary in sorrow
Patiently awaits
A return
That will never be;

Tears have dried
From the ravaged eyes
Of a grief-stricken sweetheart,
Who, like an ethereal flower
Withered in tragedy,
Sadly mourns
A love
That never
Has bloomed.

There is nothing you can do.
There is nothing they can do.
There is nothing anyone can do.

And so you lie here,
Unremembered,
A tale untold,
A soul unpitied,
A voice unheard,
A spectre unseen,
A dream unfulfilled,
A memory unpleasant.

And forever you remain,
A soldier unwept.

FOR THE MISSING IN ACTION

John Balaban

Hazed with heat and harvest dust
the air swam with flying husks
as men whacked rice sheaves into bins
and all across the sunstruck fields
red flags hung from bamboo poles.
Beyond the last treeline on the horizon
beyond the coconut palms and eucalyptus
out in the moon zone puckered by bombs
the dead earth where no one ventures,
the boys found it, foolish boys
riding buffaloes in craterlands
where at night bombs thump and ghosts howl.
A green patch on the raw earth.
And now they've led the farmers here,
the kerchiefed women in baggy pants,
the men with sickles and flails, children
herding ducks with switches—all
staring from a crater berm; silent:
In that dead place the weeds had formed a man
where someone died and fertilized the earth, with flesh
and blood, with tears, with longing for loved ones.
No scrap remained; not even a buckle
survived the monsoons, just a green creature.
a viney man, supine, with posies for eyes,
butterflies for buttons, a lily for a tongue.
Now when huddled asleep together
the farmers hear a rustly footfall
as the leaf-man rises and stumbles to them.

POW/MIA

W. D. Ehrhart

I.

In the jungle of years,
lost voices are calling. Long
are the memories,
bitterly long the waiting,
and the names of the missing and dead
wander
disembodied
through a green tangle
of rumors and lies,
gliding like shadows among vines.

II.

Somewhere, so the rumors go,
men still live in jungle prisons.
Somewhere in Hanoi, the true believers
know,
the bodies of four hundred servicemen
lie on slabs of cold
communist hate.

III.

Mothers, fathers,
wives and lovers,
sons and daughters,
touch your empty fingers to your lips
and rejoice
in your sacrifice and pain:
your loved ones' cause
was noble,
says the state.

IV.

In March of 1985, the wreckage
of a plane was found in Laos.
Little remained of the dead:
rings, bone chips, burned

bits of leather and cloth;
for thirteen families,
twenty years of hope
and rumors
turned acid on the soul
by a single chance discovery.

V.

Our enemies are legion,
says the state;
let bugles blare
and bang the drum slowly,
bang the drum.

VI.

God forgive me, but I've seen
that triple-canopied green
nightmare of a jungle
where a man in a plane could go down
unseen, and never be found
by anyone.
Not ever.
There are facts,
and there are facts:
when the first missing man
walks alive out of that green tangle
of rumors and lies,
I shall lie
down silent as a jungle shadow,
and dream the sound of insects
gnawing bones.

In Southeast Asia

Chris Taniguchi

for W. S. T., who returned

There is a large sunken field

The air is very thick and rain
falls through it slowly

The rain falls and fills the field,
feels warm and unbroken with the air
and reflects a muddy sky

In the field there is a woman in muddy rags
She is very old as this picture is old

The old woman is pushing long green stalks
into the warmed mud
at the bottom of the field

She moves slowly along the green rows
as if she's done this work forever
Her wrists and brown ankles are wet
and glisten with mud

I see you lying there, looking
up at the sky that is warm
and slow now

you try to raise your beautiful face
to me but the old woman gently
pushes you back down
and pins your face in the mud
with a slender green stalk and slowly

goes on planting the field

RETURNING THE MISSING

Lamont Steptoe

Boxes
smaller than bodies
returning the missing home
Dogtags
and wood
fragments of bone
All that's left
of Johnny
Jimmy
Jose
Leroy
Willie
or Jake
All that's left
of history
impassioned mystery
sundown
of mistake

At the Vietnam Veterans Memorial, Washington, D.C.: Chrissie

Eugene E. Grollmes

In the shade of a maple. She
Sits on the ground. At a distance
From the wall—looking at a
Name she knows is there.
Her father's. Killed near Khe
Sanh. Two months before she
Was born. Sixteen years ago.
"You look exactly like him,"
She is told. And she does—
She knows from her mother's
Photo-album. But today she
Sits contemplating his love for
Her. Her love for him.
So much a part of her.
Growing-up. Beautiful. But
Without his seeing her,
Holding her . . . without
Hearing him call her name.
The handsome First Lieutenant . . .
Who would have been so
Proud of her. Her dad.

MIDNIGHT AT
THE VIETNAM VETERANS MEMORIAL

W. D. Ehrhart

Fifty-eight thousand American dead,
average age: nineteen years, six months.
Get a driver's license,
graduate from high school,
die.
All that's left of them
we've turned to stone.
What they never got to be
grows dimmer by the year.

But in the moon's dim light
when no one's here,
the names rise up, step down
and start the long procession home
to what they left undone,
to what they loved, to anywhere
that's not this silent
wall of kids, this
smell of rotting dreams.

AT THE VIETNAM MEMORIAL

George Bilgere

The last time I saw Paul Castle
it was printed in gold on the wall
above the showers in the boys'
locker room, next to the school
record for the mile. I don't recall
his time, but the year was 1968
and I can look across the infield
of memory to see him on the track,
legs flashing, body bending slightly
beyond the pack of runners at his back.

He couldn't spare a word for me,
two years younger, junior varsity,
and hardly worth the waste of breath.
He owned the hallways, a cool blonde
at his side, and aimed his interests
further down the line than we could guess.

Now, reading the name again,
I see us standing in the showers,
naked kids beneath his larger,
comprehensive force—the ones who trail
obscurely, in the wake of the swift,
like my shadow on this gleaming wall.

A Vietnam Veteran's Memorial Day
Bill Bauer

We weep today for those
whose names are carved on this wall,
for those whose bodies
tumble in distant waters,
for those who've never returned
from the dust of another country.

We weep too for these old soldiers
standing here to the boom of the guns
and the haunted brass of bitter bugles.
They empty their tears for themselves,
for the lies they believed,
for the boys they once were
before they learned to kill.

At the Vietnam Wall
Duong Tuong

because i never knew you
nor did you me
                    i come
because you left behind mother, father
                              and betrothed
and i wife and children
                    i come
because love is stronger than enmity
and can bridge oceans
                    i come
because you never return
and i do
                    i come

Washington, D.C., November 21, 1995

Unveiling the Vietnam Memorial

Fran Castan

In the failing light, survivors
found the name they sought
cut in the polished stone
and they stroked it
as if it were a person.
I watched on television,
far from that monument, far
from your grave.
If I do nothing
to release myself from this pain,
I will never forget you.
In the village of my body,
I, too, am a burn victim,
draped in wet skin.
And I will be buried as you were,
unhealed, as were the others—
Americans and Vietnamese.

Remember our dog?
She rolled in feathers, in leaves,
even dried turds—anything
to disguise herself, to stalk her prey.
How did we learn
to make a monument to some
and to call others enemy,
to conceal our species from itself
With the body of each warrior
we place in the earth,
we etch ourselves most truly
into the cold memory of stone: the acid
history of our kind, which murders its own.

THE WALL
Horace Coleman/Shaka Aku Shango

This simple place
etched with graffiti
naming the dead
was designed by the daughter of
a woman I know
who tried with her husband
to keep their child safe
from political opinions and controversy
not knowing the young woman
would be the architect
of hatred
frustration
envy

and a healing blackness

The Peace Monument

Jan Barry

When will people put up statues to those
who kept the peace? Honor
those who sacrificed to stop the slaughter?

When will hometowns list local heroes who refused
to join the last great lust for killing
when it swept half the world like a plague?

Where are the statues to those brave souls
who kept the peace, however much provoked
by those who make a profession of destruction?

War monuments do not commemorate any peace
but that of blasted battlefields, blasted bodies,
blasted dreams.

Where are the village green and city park monuments
to those who kept the greens? To those
who kept the parks' peace?

> Listen:
> Death is a goddamned disgrace.
> It has no respect
> for beauty or for wit
> or for a lifetime
> of survivor's experience—
> so why should I show
> any respect for it?
>> Death will catch me
>> in due time,
>> but until then
>> the time is mine.

WHITE WALL

Rod McQueary

There ought to be another wall
White, bright, pretty
In a grove of trees
    with picnic tables,
    dance floor, and a
Viet Vet ragtime band.
A happy place where
    Folks could go to laugh
    and dance and argue
Football teams and candidates.
On the White Wall, there would be
A tremendous list of those
    Who didn't die.
Behind each name,
    a little heart . . . for a fulfilling marriage
    a little happy face . . . for a
    well-adjusted child,
    a little diploma . . . for a valuable education,
    a rewarding life.

Everyone is welcome here,
To cool drinks, rummy games,
To meet interesting people who
Talk, laugh, have fun, wander off.
    Live
To celebrate our survivorhood.
Not mourn our stolen martyrdom.

There are some who will
Have to be shown
The White Wall.
Taken to their own name
and told
"There, by God, is proof."

Miles of Bones
Bill Shields

58,000 suicides
is a lot of bullets

wrecked car's
ruined veins

dead bottles
kids without fathers

American flags

& miles of dirt dug

58,000
the number of Vietnam

veteran suicides . . .
it equals the names

on the Wall
today: 7/09/91 8:10 p.m.

tomorrow
we'll exceed it

more suicide
than combat death

If you can't feel
this pain

you're already
dead

all these
bodies

floating
home

MOTHER'S PEARLS

Bao-Long Chu

Broken shadow gestured winter
trees in Maine, black on white
I thought of my mother's pearls,
ebony seeds, old as the sea
They lie
suspended from her white ao dai
   The color of mourning
   or of mornings in 1975
   unbroken, silent
   after a rain of bombs
   except for the tears of women
   crying for broken temples against green
   sky; fallen idols
   with carved breasts,
   jade, I think, in the black earth,
   in the twisted vines

Last summer, in Washington
I saw the black wall
My shadow reflected
the names of faceless men.
I traced the ruins
carved in stone but did not find
Mother's name
or the names of other women
who stood against the wall of a temple
garden, parting leaves, weeping
napalm tears
   Sandalwood incense
   sweet crooked smoke
they drove all things
out of mind.
And the pearls
forty seeds, black and unruly,
I thought they were beautiful against
my mother's carved breasts.

They lie now,
I think, on a sloping knoll
farther than Maine
or Washington.

10

Lost in a Foreign Silence

History

Thuong Vuong-Riddick

From China, the Yuen people traveled south, and killed
the Thai, the Khmers, the Mongs and the Chams from the
kingdom of Funan. As a result of their "Marching towards
the South," the Yuen became independent, the Viet.

Then for ten centuries the Chinese waged war and killed
the Vietnamese and called Vietnam, Annam, which means
"The Pacified South."

The French killed the Vietnamese and
occupied the country for a century.
The Vietnamese who fought the French
were called Vietminh.
The French and the Vietnamese killed
the Vietminh (secretly helped by the Americans).

The Japanese killed the French.
The Japanese allied with the French killed
the Chinese and the Vietminh.
The Japanese helped the Vietnamese to proclaim
the Independence of Vietnam.
The Japanese killed the French and were defeated.
The Americans helped the Vietminh to become
the Democratic Republic of Vietnam.
The French and their allies, the British,
killed the Vietminh.
The French equipped by the Americans lost to
the Vietminh, equipped by the Chinese.
The Americans took the place of the French.
The Vietminh were called the Vietcong.

The Vietcong armed by China and the U.S.S.R.
killed the Vietnamese and the Americans.
The Vietcong prevailed.

People fled overseas.

LETTER FROM BAC NINH, WRITTEN TO A BROTHER IN AMERICA

Bao-Long Chu

Last night, thunderous shapes
crossed my window to the world.
Sweetness burned in the nose.

Father woke with a start,
told me all are poor signs,
his terrible bed sighed, darkened.

This morning, I found bones
in the risen water of our well.

Brother, after all these years, bones
of the unmourned still float back home.

The years have cleansed them.
I buried them next to the mangosteen
tree we named after you.

We did what you would.
We scattered flowers so this one
will not forget the sweetest scent.

*The dead remember, the living
forget*, Father insisted.

I turned the soil. I kissed the bones.
I lay down in the earth

Sodden from rain, I heard the tamarind
trees moaning their diurnal secrets,
their desire for nothing, for no one.

I write to you from among the dead,
the dead floating in rain,
the dead longing for return,

the dead remembering another
season, another named tree,

the palsied dead, the insisted dead,
the lingered dead, the sweetened dead,

the dead whose leaving is far, Older
Brother, the lovely dead who speaks
in weeping as you did at the ocean's edge.

M.I.A.

Bao-Long Chu

When you come back,
don't bother to

go to Cho-lon.
I am not there
among mangoes

I once peddled.
I am here now:

America.
Yes, I wait still.
Still, as Buddha.

I wake early
daily to make

you lotus soup
you love, thinking
you will today

break down this house
when you come back

and find me, love,
breaking, broken,
into ashes.

The green seas stretch,
but they're not end-

less. If you are
lost, please follow
my skin, my faith.

I burn nightly.

UMBILICAL CORD

Tu-Uyen Nguyen

You lift the pearl-lacquered lid
Revealing a ballerina figurine
Spinning spinning spinning round.
Her static dance to the boxed piano music
Reflected in the dusty square mirror

Two small packages of white gauze
Nestled against the dark blood velvet
Sit quietly waiting my gaze

"When we escaped from Vietnam,"
You say as you reach out
Your hands
"I secretly brought this on the boat."

You slowly unwrap the cloth as
Though the fragile threads might
Crumble from your fingers' kneading and
Unravel all the memories kept
So safely tucked away for
Over a decade of pain

"When you and your brother were born
I asked the doctor to keep
Your innocent umbilical cords"

You had dried the living strands
Underneath the Vietnam sun
Until they had shriveled into
Themselves, two threads of memories

And as the patterned years passed
The threads were sewn, woven
Loosely, they now tell me stories
About that place where I was born so
Late nights I would dream of
A prior life intangible as blood
Stains streaked across the white gauze

Do you still remember Vietnam?
The memories ask me what
You cannot, are afraid to
Find that much more has been severed
Than just the umbilical cord

Shattered lives, uprooted
From the land
Left constantly floating
Like the boat we drifted in
For six days and seven nights

"Maybe someday, you will see
Vietnam and what was left behind
Your disrupted childhood re-woven."

You close the lid.
The ballerina stops spinning.
And we are left
To think from memory to memory

SAIGON: THE UNHEALED WOUND

Minh Vien

In the vast ocean of history, I'm a small sailboat
Burdened with grief from the Fall of Saigon:
An Unhealed Wound, aching and bleeding in my soul
For ten freezing years in exile

Being ragged under the stormy sky
I venture into Freedom upon a heavy strange sea
Where mankind's sorrows are large waves
        moving up and down
And the lonesome boat confuses the seaways

Shedding mournful tears, I'm exhausted, a tattered kite,
        solitary,
Faraway, my Dear, you're the shade of a lean tree
Do you miss me, an adventurous cloud
Separated from its forests and mountains for ten years?

I'm proud of being Vietnamese
With dark sparkling eyes and flat nose of the yellow race,
        forever ...
When I pass away, if there is no land for a grave,
Oh sea! Let fish devour my corpse
        But let my soul be free eternally ...

Appearing vaguely in the day, but clearly in my dreams
        at night,

Saigon becomes vivid in my mind ...

As a tree belongs to its roots,
I owe Saigon so many thanks
For a blue moon youth
And a rosy sun manhood:
Full of flowery dreams in a lovely city
I enter the world enthusiastically ...

Oh Saigon, we lose each other!
With a withered heart and a worn-out body,
I have lived joylessly away from you,
        my poetic lover and my friends for ten years

My soul will carry this sorrow
Until I pay the debt of nature . . .

Oh my Dear! Remembering Dakao
I miss your summery starlit eyes
Remembering the Thi Nghè River,
I miss your long black hair's shadow
          swimming in it

Remembering the Saigon Zoo,
I miss the cicadas' concerts
          in the summer afternoons
Remembering Trung Vuong High School,
I miss you, a dreamy white butterfly
          with the sweet voice of an oriole . . .
Missing you, I remember our tearful kiss
At a heart breaking separation!
Now you're alone in our ravaged country,
A pitiful half-life of me . . .

Oh Saigon! Are you different from yesterday?
Ten years, it's hard to believe, already have flown away!
I still remember my friends in the open-air restaurant
On Nguyen Tri Phuong Street, one dying afternoon
Got drunk with Music and Poetry
At my farewell party
And when the party was over
We said goodbye in smoky voices to each other . . .
Now, missing my friends, on a strange sea
I cry for their dark life silently! . . .
Oh Saigon! I remember that last rainy night:
The deserted Six-City Bus Station had a dim light.
Waiting for a bus to take me out of town,
I sat quietly in a small coffee shop
And drank many cups of the bitterness of a lonely life
And smoked a lot of cigarettes
Which nearly burnt my dry lips and sour tongue . . .
Then, when getting into a bus for the departure,
I wept bitterly like rain
And waved to you and said goodbye . . .
My soul has been in pain
As if our separation happened yesternight! . . .

Oh Saigon! Are you still mine?
Though close in my mind, you're far away,
        thousands of miles! . . .

As long as I live in exile,
Saigon will be the Unhealed Wound aching in my soul day
and night! . . .

Shrapnel Shards on Blue Water

Le Thi Diem Thuy

To My Sister Le Thi Diem Trinh

everyday i beat a path to run to you
beaten into the meeting snow/the telephone poles
which separate us like so many signals of slipping time
and signposts marked in another language
my path winds and unwinds, hurls itself toward you
until it unfurls before you
all my stories at your feet
rocking against each other like marbles
down a dirt incline
listen

ma took the train every morning
sunrise
from phan thiet to saigon
she arrived
carrying food to sell at the markets
past sunset
late every evening she carried her empty baskets
home
on the train which runs in the opposite direction
away from the capital
toward the still waters of the south china sea

once ba bought an inflatable raft
yellow and black
he pushed it out onto a restricted part of water
in southern california
after midnight

to catch fish in the dark
it crashed against the rocks
he dragged it back to the van
small and wet
he drove us home
our backs turned in shame
from the pacific ocean

our lives have been marked by the tide
every day it surges forward
hits the rocks
strokes the sand
turns back into itself again
a fisted hand

know this about us
we have lived our lives
on the edge of oceans
in anticipation of
sailing into the sunrise
i tell you all this
it tears apart the silence
of our days and nights here

i tell you all this
to fill the void of absence
in our history
here

we are fragmented shards
blown here by a war no one wants to remember
in a foreign land
with an achingly familiar wound
our survival is dependent upon
never forgetting that vietnam is not
a word
a world
a love
a family
a fear
to bury

let people know
VIETNAM IS NOT A WAR

let people know
VIETNAM IS NOT A WAR

let people know
VIETNAM IS NOT A WAR
but a piece of
us,
sister
and
we are
so much

more

Tet in America
Tran Thi Nga

The whole week of Tet
I prepared our favorite dishes
three times a day every day.
After the incense burned,
I removed the food from the altar,
put it on the table.

How silly I felt each noontime
alone in my house
surrounded by little saucers of food,
no one to share them with
no neighbors around me celebrating.

I'd asked my children to take time off
the way I had.
They said, "What for?
So we can sit around the table
and stare at each other?"

I said I did this not for them
but for our ancestors.
Inside I was sad
feeling myself on a desert
knowing my customs will die with me.

BLUES

Thuong Vuong-Riddick

Coming from the tropics,
the hardest for me in the Paris winter:
not to live
in the daylight.

Days so short
they could not be appreciated.

This panic:
my life being engulfed
in an endless tunnel of the night.

I never imagined
Paris as a gray old woman,
the endless avenues,
metro travel,
the boredom of Sorbonne classes,
loud university restaurants,
endless forms for a single book.

I browse in the bookstores,
meet friends in the coffee shops.
We speak of Jean-Luc Godard,
Eisenstein, Bergman, Antonioni.

Outside of Vietnam,
Paris, largest Vietnamese city
in the world,
clans formed again.

I began to read about the war,
weary of separating the world
into bad and good
knowing that
every moment
someone fell beneath
a burst of gunfire.

Both sides using the same methods
to justify the slaughter
of a population

they claim to protect
or wish
to set free.

Three generations were sacrificed
so many mowed down
in the prime of life.

But no one today
can see our wounds.

Use an X ray
to photograph our souls—
you will glimpse
a landscape
incomprehensible
even to ourselves.

HOME

Thien-bao Thuc Phi

Da Lat streets unroll onto my pillow
its citizens stir with the first fogs, 5am,
get up to jog by Ho Xuan Huong
while I dream, hidden deep under swirling Minnesota
    blizzards.
You are too young to remember these things.
I don't know that I am being buried alive, under the cold.
Time crawls down a stick of incense,
leaving behind ash, the sweet smell of burning
led by red ember glows, sun over green rice field dreams.
You must remember what home means.
My dreams do not leave tracks in the snow, for others to
    follow.
A water buffalo with no one on its back
wanders deep into my life
walks past me, does not look back.
These are the things you left behind.

This Is the House I Pass Through Daily

Bao-Long Chu

My mother
takes sharp stones and builds a house with many rooms
    through which she wanders nightly,
        her insomnia,

a lighted
candle that guides her hand, casts her body from room
    to room. This house, this dream, like
        the boat that floated

our bodies
here, is filled with secrets that leave me open,
    open like the sea that was
        promise, like the scent

of lilacs
I imagined because on that boat we were flesh
    to flesh, because my mother
        breathed hard, clutched my hand

every time
a man came to her. Her body saved me. Not milk.
    Not food. And not my father,
        who came after us,

not knowing
how my mother wanders from him, how I stand guard
    over this house she has made
        smooth from such sharp stones.

THREE-LETTER WORD

Mong Lan

Taking praying and waiting as a vocation
and training myself in the awful art of wanting nothing
I have earthed then unearthed the _ _ _
that was the one smoldering fact of our lives, the prime gap
I haven't been able to forget (or remember entirely)
for the events emanate from it as everything
emanates from 0 and goes forwards or backwards
as time crouches with moon-lizard eyes,
I've felt fire burn in my throat and that fire was History
        unmade, History
in the making; one early morning one hundred armies
        marched
through my esophagus, some used spears and guns and rocks
and a few used chemicals and atomic power, but the truth of
        the matter
was, no one wanted to be there, that was the _ _ _we don't
want to think about,
those who lived during it and after it, who ate the rationed
        rice, used the rationed
spools of thread, rationed needles (three per family), rationed
        gruel, fuel,
and rationed love in the rationed space, know this: Akhmatova
was right when she said _ _ _s make Shakespearean tragedies
        child's play, _ _ _
dirty word (of generations), like the slick black oil that slips
through our hands as easily as the named deaths and
        unnamed
deaths on the slick black wall in Arlington, the age is ill if the
        angels
in our nightmares don't warn us our destinies,
let the one hundred and one origami seagulls fly from coast
to coast carrying possibilities, a whole generation of husband
        less
women in Vietnam, their childhood sweethearts dead because
        of the _ _ _ unmarried
because of the _ _ _ pitied and solitary because of the _ _ _
        and waiting

for the next life to marry, they've almost gone to dyeing their
 teeth despair-red,
irrational time doesn't let me forget, nonlinear time
corners me into places and openings in which all the axes
convened: monkey-howling darkness of brain-plashed jungles,
 shelter
in the brimming seas, flames firing
in stones, hope cultivated in waiting, smoke of headaches,
 hustled love,
caffeinic love / this poem speaks of the light around the 0 that
 is _ _ _
the light dimmed when the _ _ _ went on, the murky
light of those who live in mute verse
for these stone-shaped words were meant to be swallowed
one by one wading in cradles of incense or standing on the arc
of an infinite numinous ocean.

How I Could Interpret the Events of my Youth, Events I Do Not Remember Except in Dreams

Christian Nguyen Langworthy

Because I was a newly adopted
        child from another country,
(a prostitute's son in a Vietnamese
        city bristling with rifles
and as a result of my mother's truancy
        from motherhood I was given
to nuns and locked within the confines
        of missionary walls)
I crossed the perilous South China Sea
        and Pacific in three days
(barely surviving anti-aircraft fire)
        aboard an eight prop-engine plane.
I came to this country
        to a nine-inch carpet of snow
and a sure welcome by strangers
        engaged with the possibilities of parenthood.

My new beginning consisted of firsts:
        first experienced snowfall in America—
(how it was magic in a fairy tale land)
        first toilet flushings,
(at the airport, when I flushed every
        toilet in the men's room to my new
father's delight)
        and another notable first—
the first cartoon I ever saw on Saturday
        morning: Bugs Bunny and Elmer Fudd,
and how there were no wounded or dead
        from the flying bullets,
and I laughed so hard I cried
        though I did not understand their language then.

As the years of my second life progressed,
        my adopted parents tried so to be
a good father and mother and to the cinema
        we went, and I saw the children's epics:

Snow White and the Seven Dwarfs
     and Sleeping Beauty; at home my mother read
fairy tales to me, tales like Rumpelstiltskin,
     and I learned
the false beauty of the wicked witch,
     the castle besieged by thorns,
the terror of the kidnapped son.
     I could have told them I'd seen these tales
before, but I was too young to know the difference.

Bui Doi 7

R. A. Streitmatter/Tran Trong Dat

I sometimes say
My whole village was killed
I sometimes say
I still have family left in Viet Nam
I sometimes say
She's still searching for me.

But I know
That she did not want me.
I know
That I was more mistake than son.
I know
that in the absence of fact

I can only sometimes say.

Bui Doi

R. A. Streitmatter/Tran Trong Dat

Where to begin
Speaking to you is like speaking to a ghost
If your intent was my safe arrival to the United States,
You've succeeded.

Resentment for having abandoned me
Leaving legacies of questions unanswered.
Resentment for having no history, no blood.
Resentment for being so selfish as not to leave a note,
A picture, a memento of you.
Resentment that I haven't an idea who you are.

The war, the G.I.'s, you and I.
Who do I blame?
Tell me mother, how is it that I came to be?
Do you call yourself Nguoi Viet?
My father: Vietnamese, French, Chinese or American?
Was it Love or prostitution?

Are you aware of my existence and my loss?
Will there be reunion in Heaven?
You had given me life
Yet stolen everything I have.

Were we ever to meet
I would be speechless,
Unsure whether I'd cry or remain indifferent,
Undecided whether I would abandon you in return
Or embrace you with my infant arms for eternity.
I shall never know answers.
You saw to that.

Leaving me nameless, worthless dust,
Without a birthdate,
Without a clue as to who you are.
I don't know why
But I'm still searching for you
Because without you
I'll never know myself.

Dui Boi, DUST OF LIFE

Yusef Komunyakaa

You drifted from across the sea
under a carmine moon,
framed now in my doorway
by what I tried to forget.
Curly-headed & dark-skinned,
you couldn't escape
eyes taking you apart.
Come here, son, let's see
if they castrated you.

Those nights I held your mother
against me like a half-broken
shield. The wind's refrain
etched my smile into your face—
is that how you found me?
You were born disappearing.
You followed me, blameless
as a blackbird in Hue
singing from gutted jade.

Son, you were born with dust
on your eyelids, but you bloomed up
in a trench where stones were
stacked to hold you down.
With only your mother's name,
you've inherited the inchworm's
foot of earth. *Dui boi.*
I blow the dust off my hands
but it flies back in my face.

Between Thumb and Index Finger
Truong Tran

between thumb and index finger   hold a rat by the neck
gentle firm   pull the tail once   listen for the snap   painless
quick   skinned fried   the difference in taste   there is none
at twenty three   barefooted   bullet in his thigh   my cousin
was forced   into camp   re-education   real   *the table legs*
immerse   into four bowls of water   hunger begins with   a
trail
of red ants   at twenty three   I am taught by this cousin
how to accent   words   *hold a pen   as you would chopsticks*
gentle   let it rest   between thumb   and index finger

Tombstones
Mong Lan

In the region of destruction, ideas are felt and given birth:
my family name echoes on the tombstones
like rock skipping on water, like a blind creed

Consciousness tells me that
I am here on this field in Vietnam, not California
not Texas, not Mexico City nor Paris

that where light streams on the verdant paddy fields
    children run and play with the same savagery as any-
where
    as hundreds of years ago, as hundreds of years hence
that the dark young men carrying piles of straw large as
    horses
      will never know the touch of an IBM or Macintosh, that
      these young
    men and women know something that we lack
that the texture of soil, texture of broken earth feels different
    in the hands of a father of six than in the hands of a
    father of two
      that the mist of my ancestors rising embrace the slow
      keel
    of the earth

that the stories Father told us about his water buffalo days
    weren't fabricated, and indeed
        here is his childhood comrade speaking to him with
        watery eyes
            that the thatched houses, piles of hay, rarefied air of
            tombs speak to the children as they
        play and grow older and the children in turn will speak to
        them
            that these children of hay will claim their ancestors land
            as the land claims them
                that the family name on tombstones become a creed
                handed down, forever passed down

consciousness tells me that
this is what it means to endure with the land
this is what it means to worship ancestors
this is what it means to have the earth claim you.

WAITING FOR A CYCLO IN THE HOOD

Thien-bao Thuc Phi

26th Street, a one way,
flows by my house, keeps going right
out of the hood, before spilling into
Uptown: fertile delta of the young,
disturbingly hip, rich by no fault of their own,
nothing to do on a Saturday night but be beautiful.
I sit on the curb, far from lovely,
empty pocket's distance from rich,
wishing I knew
which way to go.
Back in Viet Nam I could
shout for a Cyclo, hold up a fist of small dong,
peel each dollar from the tension of my hand
and let them fly away to the Doppler Effect,
one by one,
scream the words to Prince's "1999" in two languages
and not once look behind me to see
if the cyclo driver was whispering:

this street is one way, I can't take you back
to where you came from, no matter how many American
dollar bills you give up
to the wind.

FOR MRS. NA
Cu Chi District
December 1985

W. D. Ehrhart

I always told myself,
if I ever got the chance to go back,
I'd never say "I'm sorry"
to anyone. Christ,

those guys I saw on television once:
sitting in Hanoi, the cameras rolling,
crying, blubbering
all over the place. Sure,

I'm sorry. I never meant
to do the things I did.
But that was nearly twenty years ago:
enough's enough.

If I ever go back,
I always told myself,
I'll hold my head steady
and look them in the eye.

But here I am at last—
and here you are.
And you lost five sons in the war.
And you haven't any left.
And I'm staring at my hands
and eating tears,
trying to think of something else to say
besides "I'm sorry."

A CONICAL HAT
for Lê Cao Dài and Vu Giáng Huong

Kevin Bowen

A moment of awkwardness
as he bends to lift the gift
to the table, not as if
he could hide it, the broad
conical shape of the *"non la"*
stared up at us all through dinner,
the girl who served us
stepping around it
as if to draw attention all the more.

Across the table all night
I watch the stories
come alive in his eyes;
I can almost see the bulb burning;
a man pedals a bicycle underground,
in the shadows of the bunker
he makes power for lights and suction
in the operating room.
Lungs burn, he inhales
fine red bits of earth.
They are digging to expand the tunnels,
make more room for the wounded.

A figure in white
draws a suture through
last bits of skin,
prays his sight holds.
One day he walks
straight off the earth,
right into the brown, wrinkled
hide of an elephant,
carves meat for a starving platoon,
takes machete and scalpel,
makes cut after cut
until he's covered
in blood and muscle,
fighting for air.

1970. A break in the fighting.
A game of volleyball, interrupted.
A gunship sprays the pitch.
Two nurses killed, he drags
their bodies down, heavy
and smoking, into the tunnels.

Ten years, his wife
slept in mountain caves,
after bombs, repaired roads,
made posters, paintings
to record each detail.

"Ham Rong Bridge, 1970," he shows me.
A woodcut on rice paper.
Two women in conical hats
load rocks along a road.

In the background trucks
grow wings of camouflage,
rattle across the bridge
heading south.

His eyes burn as he looks
through the woodcut.
I thank him. I will need this hat,
the cool circle of its shade.

Her Life Runs Like a Red Silk Flag

Bruce Weigl

Because this evening Miss Hoang Yen
sat down with me in the small
tiled room of her family house
I am unable to sleep.
We shared a glass of cold and sweet water,
On a blue plate her mother brought us
cake and smiled her betel black teeth at me
but I did not feel strange in the house
my country had tried to bomb into dust.
In English thick and dazed as blood
she told me how she watched our planes
cross her childhood's sky,
all the children of Hanoi
carried in darkness to mountain hamlets, Nixon's
Christmas bombing. She let me hold her hand,
her shy unmoving fingers, and told me
how afraid she was those days and how this fear
had dug inside her like a worm and lives
inside her still, won't die or go away.
And because she's stronger, she comforted me,
said I'm not to blame,
the million sorrows alive in her gaze.
With the dead we share no common rooms.
With the frightened we can't think straight;
no words can bring the burning city back.
Outside on Hung Dao Street
I tried to say goodbye and held her hand
too long so she looked back through traffic
towards her house and with her eyes
she told me I should leave.
All night I ached for her and for myself
and nothing I could think or pray
would make it stop. Some birds sang morning
home across the lake. In small reed boats
the lotus gatherers sailed out
among their resuming white blossoms.

Hanoi, 1990

THREE FISH

Bruce Weigl

Duc Thanh brought me three fish
    he had caught in the small lake on Nguyen Du.

They were the color of pearls;
    they were delicate and thin. Already

winter was in the wind from China,
    voices of ancestors on swan's wings.

This late in the season,
    evening traffic's hum and weave beginning to rise

beyond the guardians of the gate,
    these fish are a great gift.

I was in my room,
    lost in a foreign silence.

I wanted to eat the miles up somehow,
    I wanted to split my soul in two

so I could stay forever
    in the musty guest house pleasures.

I was that far away, that lost
    when he called to me, ghost that he is,

across the courtyard, and in moonlight,
    held up three silver fish.

A Song of My Native Village
for Chua, my native village

Nguyen Quang Thieu
> *Translated by the author and Martha Collins*

I sing a song of my native village
When everyone is deep in sleep
Under wet stars, under wild winds
Finding their way home.

Somewhere a man speaks in his sleep
Beside a woman's streaming hair;
Somewhere the smell of a mother's milk
Flows into the night;
Somewhere the breasts of girls of fifteen
Rise from the land like shoots.
And somewhere the coughs of old villagers
Fall from branches like ripe fruit
And grass wakes up lonely in the garden.

I sing a song of my native village
In the light of the oil lamp
Left by my ancestors
The loveliest and saddest of lamps.
When I was born my mother placed it
Before me that I might look and learn
To be sad, to love, and to cry.

I sing a song of my native village.
I sing through my navel cord
Which was buried there
And became an earthworm
Crawling under the water jar
Crawling by the edge of the pond
Crawling through my ancestors' graves
Crawling through the paupers' graves
Pushing up red earth in its path like blood.

I sing a song of my native village,
Bones lying in terra-cotta coffins

Where mine will lie someday.
In this life I am human;
In the next I will be an animal.
I will ask to be a little dog
To defend the sadness.
The jewel of my native village.

Untitled

Ngo Vinh Long

On this land
    Where each blade of grass is human hair
Each foot of soil is human flesh
    Where it rains blood
Hails bones
    Life must flower

What I Leave to My Son

Du Tu Le

> *Translated by Nguyen Ngoc Bich, Burton Raffel, and W. S. Merwin*

No point in leaving you a long list
of those who have died:
Even if I limit it to my friends and your uncles
it won't do. Who could remember them all?
My son, isn't it true?
The obituaries leave me indifferent
as the weather. Sometimes they seem to matter
even less: How can that be, my son?

I'll leave you, yes,
a treasure I'm always seeking, never finding.
Can you guess? Something wondrous,
something my father wanted for me
although (poor man!) it's been nothing
but a mirage in the desert
of my life.
My soul will join his now, praying
that your generation may find it—
simply peace—
simply a life better than ours
where you and your friends won't be forced
to drag grief-laden feet down the road
to mutual murder.

Peace, So That

Greg Kuzma

every stinking son of a bitch
can come home
to his lawn mower and rice paddy,
every punished son of a bitch
can return to his father's bedside,
every child of every bastard
every child of every hero of peace
of war
can talk it over with the man he blames,
every woman, mother, wife, daughter,
will rise in our arms like the tide,
every bomb be water
every bullet be smashed into frying pans,
every knife sharpened again
to cut fruit in thin slices,
every word flung out like a bullet
in anger
come back to putrefy the tongue,
every man who has sat silent
beware of his silence,
every rising of the blood
make love to a woman, a man,
every killer have only mirrors
to shoot at,
every child a thumb to suck,
every house its chance
to sink to the earth's calling,
every dead shall have no good reasons.

And we be a long time at this.

In Celebration of Spring

John Balaban

Our Asian war is over; others have begun.
Our elders, who tried to mortgage lies,
are disgraced, or dead, and already
the brokers are picking their pockets
for the keys and the credit cards.

In delta swamp in a united Vietnam,
a marine with a bullfrog for a face,
rots in equatorial heat. An eel
slides through the cage of his bared ribs.
At night, on the old battlefields, ghosts,
like patches of fog, lurk into villages
to maunder on doorsills of cratered homes,
while all across the U.S.A.
the wounded walk about and wonder where to go.

And today, in the simmer of lyric sunlight,
the chrysalis pulses in its mushy cocoon,
under the bark on a gnarled root of an elm.
In the brilliant creek, a minnow flashes
delirious with gnats. The turtle's heart
quickens its taps in the warm bank sludge.
As she chases a Frisbee spinning in sunlight,
a girl's breasts bounce full and strong;
a boy's stomach, as he turns, is flat and strong.

Swear by the locust, by dragonflies on ferns,
by the minnow's flash, the tremble of a breast,
by the new earth spongy under our feet:
that as we grow old, we will not grow evil,
that although our garden seeps with sewage,
and our elders think it's up for auction—swear
by this dazzle that does not wish to leave us—
that we will be keepers of a garden, nonetheless.

CONTRIBUTORS

Doug Anderson received the 1994 Kate Tufts Discovery Award. In 1993 he received the Emily Balch Prize for the best poems to appear in the Virginia Quarterly Review. He writes from his experiences as an army corpsman.

Margaret Atwood has published more than thirty books, including novels, poetry, and literary criticism. She lives in Toronto.

John Balaban was a civilian conscientious objector during the Vietnam War, and a field representative for the Committee of Responsibility to Save War-Injured Children. He has published nine books of poetry and prose. He has also translated Vietnamese folk poetry into English. In 1974, his first poetry book, *After Our War,* won the Lamont Award and was nominated for the National Book Award. In 1991, his *Words for My Daughter* won the National Poetry Series. In 1997, his book, *Locusts at the Edge of Summer: New and Selected Poems,* was nominated for the National Book Award. He is currently director of the MFA program in Creative Writing at the University of Miami, Coral Gables.

Bao-Long Chu was born in My Tho, Vietnam, and came to the United States in 1975. He received his MFA from the Creative Writing Program at the University of Houston. Currently he is the program director for Writers-in-the-Schools, a nonprofit organization that engages children in the pleasures of creative writing by placing professional writers in schools and community settings.

Jan Barry is a journalist based in New Jersey. He writes: "U.S. Army 5/62–5/65, Vietnam service 12/62–10/63; appointed U.S. Military Academy, resigned to become a writer. Founding president, Vietnam Veterans Against the War, 6/67–6/71. Coedited or edited three poetry anthologies about the war and is the author of the forthcoming *Earthsongs,* a collection of new and selected poems."

R. L. Barth is an instructor of English at Xavier University in Cincinnati, Ohio. As a U.S. Marine, he served as a patrol leader in the First Reconnaissance Battalion in Vietnam.

Bill Bauer served in Vietnam in 1969 in an infantry unit stationed near the Cambodian border. A native of Kansas City, Missouri, he now lives and writes in Summit County, Colorado. His most recent book of poetry, *Last Lambs,* was published by BkMk Press in 1997.

Daniel Berrigan is a writer, teacher, political activist, ordained Roman Catholic priest, and author of countless books of poetry, theology, autobiography, memoirs. Jailed for antiwar activities, 1970–72.

D. C. Berry was with the Medical Service Corps in Vietnam, 1967–68.

George Bilgere participated in a variety of antiwar activities while a student at the University of California, Riverside, in the early 1970s. His first book of poetry, *The Going,* was published in 1994 by the University of Missouri Press and received the Devins Award. He was a Fulbright Scholar in Bilboa, Spain, 1991.

Robert Bly writes: "You might mention that I was recently arrested along with some other old-time war protesters for an action protesting the manufacture of land mines here in town (Minneapolis). I also, with Galway Kinnell and Sharon Olds, a few years ago formed a group called American Writers Against the Gulf War."

Kevin Bowen was drafted and served in the First Air Cavalry Division in Vietnam from 1968 to 1969. A former Danforth Fellow and Fulbright Fellow at New College, Oxford, he earned his PhD in English literature from the State University at Buffalo. *Forms of Prayer at the Hotel Edison,* a second collection of poems from Curbstone Press, and *Mountain River: Vietnamese Poetry from the Wars 1945–1995* with Nguyen Ba Chung and Bruce Weigl from the University of Massachusetts Press, are both due out in 1998.

Hayden Carruth is a native New Englander now living in New York. He has been the editor of *Poetry,* poetry editor of *Harper's,* and an advisory editor of *Hudson Review.* His collection *The Voice That Is Great Within Us,* has been called the standard collection of twentieth-century American poetry.

L. L. Case: No biographical information is available.

Michael Casey worked for Eugene McCarthy's presidential primary campaign in New Hampshire before being drafted in the fall of 1968. He graduated from the army's military police school at Fort Gordon, Georgia, and ended his service in the American Division in Quang Ngai and Quang Tin provinces. In 1997 Adastra Press published his second book of poetry, *Milrat,* based on a New England textile mill.

Fran Castan teaches writing and literature at the School of Visual Arts in Manhattan. She and her infant daughter were living in Hong Kong with her first husband, Sam Castan, the Southeast Asia correspondent for *Look* magazine, while he covered the war in Vietnam. He was killed in 1966 in the highlands near An Khe.

Horace Coleman/Shaka Aku Shango is a Vietnam War veteran, "class of '67." Originally from Ohio, he now lives in southern California, where he works for McDonnell Douglas Aerospace.

Martha Collins was active in the antiwar movement and first began writing poetry during the war years. Her most recent book of poems, *A History of Small Life on a Windy Planet,* won the Alice Fay Di Castagnola Award and was published by the University of Georgia.

David Connolly served honorably in Vietnam with the United States Army's Eleventh Armored Cavalry Regiment. He is proud of having been and continues to be a Vietnam Veteran Against the War.

Frank Cross served in Vietnam 1969–70 as a radioman in the recon platoon. He states that when he returned from the war, "I was carrying a rucksack full of anger, guilt, hate, remorse and it almost flattened me before I handed it over. Now Jesus carries that heavy rucksack for me and I am free to serve him." He has published numerous poems about the war.

Glover Davis teaches poetry at San Diego State University. His most recent book is *Legend,* published by Wesleyan University Press. He has recently had poems accepted by the *Formalist, Southern Poetry Review, Janus,* and *Quarterly West.*

Do Tan: No biographical information is available.

Duong Tuong lives in Vietnam. He is a poet, art critic, and translator of European and American literature.

Du Tu Le: No biographical information is available.

W. D. Ehrhart enlisted in the U.S. Marines in 1966 at the age of seventeen, and fought in Vietnam with the First Battalion, First Marines, receiving a Purple Heart, two Presidential Unit Citations, and promotion to sergeant. He later became active in Vietnam Veterans Against the War. He is the author of numerous books of prose and poetry, including *Vietnam-Perkasie, Just for Laughs,* and *Carrying the Darkness,* and is currently a self-employed writer and lecturer as well as a research fellow of the American Studies Department of the University of Wales at Swansea, UK.

Liz Farrell was a friend of Timothy Clover, of College Park, Maryland, who died in Vietnam on May 22, 1968.

James Fenton was born in England, and after being educated at Oxford, served as a freelance reporter in Indochina and, later, as Southeast Asia correspondent for the *Independent*. He currently writes for the *New York Review of Books*.

David Ferguson: No biographical information is available.

Bryan Alec Floyd was born and raised in Oklahoma. He graduated with a BA in English from Seattle University, served three years in the Marine Corps, then attended the University of Virginia, and the Johns Hopkins University. He is a professor of English and humanities at Suffolk College on Long Island. He is at work on a novel, *The House of Atreus Adamson*.

Sharon Fuhrman: No biographical information is available.

Giang Nam: Cabdriver, rubber plantation worker, bookkeeper, former Vietcong guerrilla, and popular Vietnamese poet.

The late **Allen Ginsberg** was active in the antiwar movement.

Jon Forrest Glade is a native Wyomingite and a Vietnam veteran. A draftee, he served as an MOS 11-B (grunt) with the 101st Airborne in and around the A Shau Valley, leaving aboard a hospital plane about four and a half months after he arrived. He makes his living as a professional cook.

Eugene E. Grollmes first visited the Vietnam Veterans Memorial at Christmastime in 1982, shortly after its formal dedication. He has returned many times. He is a member of the administration of Saint Louis University in St. Louis, Missouri. His poems have appeared in many literary journals nationwide.

Ha Huyen Chi was born in 1935 in Ha Dong and grew up in Hanoi. He immigrated to South Vietnam alone in 1954, joined the fourteenth class of the Vietnamese National Military Academy in 1957, and escaped to the United States in 1975 after the fall of Saigon. He has published sixteen poetry collections and eight novels.

J. Vincent Hansen served in Vietnam 1966–67 as a machine gunner with the 101st Airborne Division. He is the recipient of the 1990 Loft-McKnight Award for Poetry and a finalist for the 1991 Bush Artist Fellowship in Poetry. He lives with his wife, Jan, in St. Cloud, Minnesota.

Michael S. Harper is University Professor and Professor of English at Brown University, where he has taught since 1970. He has published ten books of poetry, two of which were nominated for the National Book Award. He is coeditor of *Every Shut Eye Ain't Asleep* (New York: Little Brown, 1994), an anthology of poetry by African-Americans from 1945 to the present.

Pauline Hebert was a member of the Army Nurse Corps when she volunteered to serve in Vietnam. She arrived there just before the Tet Offensive in 1968. She served two years in Vietnam before returning to the States and to civilian nurse care. She earned an MS in nursing and a PhD in education. She currently lives in New Hampshire.

L. Russell Herman Jr. was active in the antiwar movement from 1969 onward. He is a member of the National Writers Union (UAW Local 1981, AFL-CIO).

HHT: No biographical information is available.

George Hitchcock is a veteran of World War II. He is a painter, poet, playwright, and actor. He is the author of two novels, six published plays, and eight volumes of poetry.

Hoang Lien served as a civilian governor of Central Vietnam (northernmost provinces of South Vietnam) until 1968 when he was captured by the North Vietnamese Communists and held in prison in North Vietnam for more than twelve years. He now lives in San Francisco.

Ho Chi Minh was the president of North Vietnam from 1954 until his death in September 1969.

Daniel Hoffman served as Consultant in Poetry of the Library of Congress, the appointment now designated Poet Laureate of the United States, in 1972–73. He is the author of nine books of poetry, including *Middens of the Tribe* (1995).

David Huddle served with the 25th Military Intelligence Detachment in Cu Chi, Vietnam, in 1966–67. Among his books are *Paper Boy, Only the Little Bone,* and *The Writing Habit.* He teaches at the University of Vermont and the Bread Loaf School of English.

The late **Richard Hugo** served in the army air force in World War II and flew thirty-five missions over enemy territory.

Lowell Jaeger writes that he "left the country for Sweden in 1970. Listened to the first draft lottery on Radio Free Europe—came up #13 (July 3 birth date). Returned home, won Conscientious Objector (nonreligious) status. Refused induction. Hit the road, traveled with a West Coast carnival until amnesty for resisters was declared. Two books in print: *War on War* (1988) and *Hope Against Hope* (1990)."

Bill Jones was drafted into the U.S. Marine Corps in April 1968. He served in Vietnam for eleven months, twenty-five days, and thirteen hours as an artillery forward observer with the Third Marine Division.

The late **Milton Kaplan** was a professor of English at Columbia University. He is the author of *In a Time Between Wars*.

Mark Kessinger was born in Huntington, West Virginia, and was raised in Lorain, Ohio, on the shore of Lake Erie. He attended Lorain County Community College, where he studied with Bruce Weigl, and Cleveland State University, where he studied with Alberta Turner. He has been an auto assembly line worker, racquetball pro, air traffic controller, letter carrier, and university instructor. He now lives in Spring, Texas, with his wife, Jeanne Olexen, and their five children.

Denis Knight: No biographical information is available.

Yusef Komunyakaa served in Vietnam as correspondent and editor of *The Southern Cross*. He received the Bronze Star. He has published numerous books of poetry and won the Pulitzer Prize for poetry in 1994. He currently teaches at Princeton University.

Herbert Krohn was an army doctor in the Mekong Delta in 1966–67. He has published poetry in *The Nation, Partisan Review,* and *The New Yorker,* among others. Presently, he is an emergency room doctor in the barrio of Chelsea, Massachusetts, and performs on flute and voice in the poetry-blues-jazz group Blues Cabaret.

Greg Kuzma is professor of English at the University of Nebraska. His *Selected Poems* is due from Carnegie Mellon University Press in 1998.

Ky Niem Thanh Dang: During the war, American soldiers were often surprised to find that when they overran North Vietnamese positions, they found poems mixed in with the confiscated maps and military papers. Originally held as military documents, these poems were eventually declassified, and a sample was translated by Bruce Weigl and Thanh T. Nguyen and published under the title *Poems from Captured Documents* (University of Massachusetts Press, 1994.) Three of the poems in this anthology are from that book. No further biographical information is available about the soldiers who wrote the poems.

Christian Nguyen Langworthy was born in Vietnam in 1967 with the birth name of Nguyen Van Phuong. He was adopted in April 1975 by a family in upstate New York. He has won an American Chapbook Award and an Academy of American Poets' Prize.

Wendy Wilder Larsen taught Shakespeare and Romantic poetry at the School of Pedagogy in Saigon in the 1960s, when she was married to a correspondent of *Time* magazine serving there.

Robert Lax writes: "I'm eighty-one years old now. Have been a conscientious objector to violence in all forms since infancy. My 'activism' has been limited to writing and publishing poems, daybooks, notes and fables since the age of eleven."

McAvoy Layne served in Vietnam with the U.S. Marine Corps, 1966–67. He is the author of *How Audie Murphy Died in Vietnam* and *Hooked on Twain.*

Le Dan: No biographical information is available.

Sharon Lee wrote "Letter from Nam" for her brother, who survived the war. She is a poet and small-press editor in Dublin, California.

Le Minh Thu: No biographical information is available.

Le Thi Diem Thuy was born in South Vietnam. She and her father left in 1978, by boat, and they eventually settled in southern California. She is a writer and performer who has been touring *Mua He Do Lua/ Red Fiery Summer,* a one-woman show about Vietnam, since January 1995. Her essay "The Gangster We Are All Looking For" appeared in *Best American Essays '97.* She is currently working on a memoir by the same name, which will be published by Knopf/Vintage in 1999.

Le Thi May: No biographical information is available.

The late **Denise Levertov** wrote of her Vietnam War protest poetry: "Glancing at these pieces I feel wistful in recalling the sense of imminent social change which at that time energized so many of us. I wasn't all that young at the time but I still had a youthful fervor that's conspicuous by its absence today even in those who are young. I don't despair but I do see how very much longer everything takes and how much more complex all these issues are."

Philip Levine was born in Detroit and moved to California at the age of thirty, where he still lives. He was for some time the head of the Fresno Resistance, a support group for men who refused military service. He has written sixteen books of poetry.

Jack Lindeman served three years in the army during World War II, and was active in the movement to end the Vietnam War. He has published two books, *Twenty-one Poems* (Atlantis Editions) and *The Conflict of Convictions* (The Chilton Book Company.)

Jacqueline M. Loring is a poet who lives with her husband and large family on the west coast of Cape Cod. Her husband served in the U.S. Army, 3rd MASH Hospital in Vietnam in the Delta from Christmas of 1967 to Christmas of 1968. They have been married twenty-eight years. Her poetry and stories describe the struggle of American families to survive the effects of the Vietnam War.

Don Luce spent thirteen years in Vietnam, 1958–71, as director of International Voluntary Services in Vietnam and with the World Council of Churches. He has coauthored several books on the Vietnam War.

Luu Trong Lu, a well-known poet in the northern part of Vietnam, wrote primarily during the period of the war against French occupation.

Clarence Major is the author of ten collections of poetry, including *New and Selected Poems, 1958–1998* (Copper Canyon Press, 1998). His poetry has earned a Pushcart Prize and been published in more than two hundred periodicals. His best-selling anthology, *The New Black Poetry,* was published in 1969. He teaches African-American literature, American poetry, and creative writing at the University of California, Davis.

Paul Martin has published his poetry widely in journals, including *Green Mountains Review, Southern Humanities Review,* and *Kansas Quarterly.* His first collection, *Green Tomatoes,* was published by Heatherstone Press, and his second, *Closing Distances,* was twice a finalist in the National Poetry Series and is looking for a publisher. His brother, John, served in the Vietnam War.

Herbert Woodward Martin is a poet in residence at the University of Dayton and the Paul Laurence Dunbar Laureate Poet for the City of Dayton. He is the author of four volumes of poetry.

Steve Mason, a combat veteran and a former U.S. Army captain, is the National Poet Laureate of the Vietnam Veterans of America and serves on the national advisory board of the Veterans for Peace. He serves on the international board of advisers of the East Meets West Foundation, which builds hospitals in Vietnam. He is presently working on a new book, *At the Heart of the Dream,* dealing with the problems faced by the American workforce.

Gerald McCarthy was born in Endicott, New York, in 1947. After serving in Vietnam with the marines, he deserted and spent some time in military prison. Upon his discharge, he was active in Vietnam Veterans Against the War. He has had three books published. Currently, he is an associate professor of English at St. Thomas Aquinas College in New York.

Norman A. McDaniel participated in the Vietnam War as an EB–66C aircrew member. He was shot down over North Vietnam in July 1966 and spent nearly seven years as a prisoner of war. He retired as a colonel after twenty-eight and a half years' active duty in the U.S. Air Force. He is currently serving as a professor of systems acquisition management at the Defense Systems Management College.

Walter McDonald is poet in residence and director of the creative writing program at Texas Tech University. He was a pilot in the U.S. Air Force and served in Vietnam. He has a PhD from the University of Iowa and has published fifteen collections of poetry.

Rod McQueary left a cowboy job to join the Marine Corps in June of 1970. School trained as a rifleman, he was sent to Vietnam immediately after training, and was reassigned to the First Marine Division Military Police. He lives quietly at home near Deeth, Nevada, with his sweetheart and their herd of kids. He owns an Internet representation firm, The Cowboy Cattle-log: Premier Purveyor of the Authentic West on the Internet, at www.cattle-log.com.

W. S. Merwin lives in Hawaii. He has won the Yale series of Younger Poets Award, the Pulitzer Prize in poetry, and the Fellowship of the Academy of American Poets.

Jeff Miller was one of the students killed at Kent State on May 4, 1970.

Minh Dung: No biographical information is available.

Minh Vien was born in 1940 in Bac-Ninh, North Vietnam, and immigrated to Saigon in 1954. Formerly a teacher of Vietnamese literature and an army officer, he came to the United States in 1975 after the fall of Saigon. He now lives in San Francisco. His Internet address is http://www.poets.com/Minh-Vien.html.

L. Dean Minze: No biographical information is available.

Mong Lan was born in Saigon during the Vietnam War, and is now a writer and visual artist in Portland, Oregon. Her poetry has been included in numerous anthologies and journals.

Ngo Vinh Long served as a military mapmaker in South Vietnam from 1959 to 1963. After coming to America in 1964, he became active in the antiwar movement. He is currently professor of Asian studies at the University of Maine.

Nguyen Chi Thien was born in Hanoi in 1933. He spent a total of eighteen years in jail for anti-Communist activity. He won the Rotterdam Poetry Prize in 1985 and the Amnesty International Prize in Poetry in December 1991. He now lives in Virginia.

Nguyen Dinh Thi: No biographical information is available.

Nguyen Ngoc Phuong died in a South Vietnamese prison on January 5, 1973, after a hunger strike. He was arrested in 1970 for protesting the Saigon regime.

Nguyen Quang Thieu was born in 1957 in a village near Hanoi. He was just graduating from high school when the "American War" ended. He has published five books of poems in Vietnam, as well as several novels. He lives in Hanoi, where he is editor-in-chief of the literary magazine *Van Nghe Tre.*

Nguyen Quóc Vinh was born in Saigon in 1968 of parents who had between them nearly two decades of service with USIS and USAID. He spent his formative years in direct witness of the aftermath of the Vietnam War until his family immigrated to the United States in 1985. Entering Harvard University two years later, he received his AB in East Asian Languages and Civilizations (1991), AM in Regional Studies—East Asia (1993–94), and is presently a doctoral candidate specializing in late premodern Vietnamese literary and cultural history.

Lt. Nguyen van Nghia served in the North Vietnamese Army during the war. In 1968, poetry and journals he left behind on a battlefield were found by a young Texan GI named Paul Reed. Mr. Reed's efforts to return the lieutenant's belongings to him are detailed in his 1996 book *Kontum Diary.*

On May 16, 1967, **Nhat Chi Mai,** a teacher and worker in the Buddhist School of Social Work in Saigon, died from self-immolation.

Nhat Hanh: No biographical information is available.

Jim Nye served with the 2/502D, 101ˢᵗ ABN as a platoon leader in 1966–67. In 1969–70 he was with Command and Control South. Fifth Group, Special Forces.

Sharon Olds was born in San Francisco. She has published five books of poetry, including *The Dead and the Living,* which won the National Book Critics Circle Award. She teaches in the creative writing program at New York University.

Grace Paley writes: "I was an activist opposed to the war from 1961 on, when I first understood something not good was happening. In 1969 I was sent by the peace movement to North Vietnam—Hanoi—with several others to bring back 3 POWs. This was an American agreement with the Vietnamese to return these men home. While there we traveled the length of North Vietnam to the DMZ and saw the destruction of cities and tiny villages and the results of what bombing could do when undertaken with such cruel, powerful intention." These reports will appear as a book of nonfiction called *As I Thought,* scheduled for 1998.

Pham Tien Duat: No biographical information is available.

Leroy V. Quintana left the University of New Mexico for the army, airborne, and went to Vietnam with the 101st, transferring to a long-range reconnaissance patrol unit. He spent a year in Vietnam (1967–68) and finished his army career at Ft. Bragg, North Carolina. He is a tenured associate professor at San Diego Mesa College.

Burton Raffel wrote, translated, and edited some sixty books. In 1991 he won the French-American Foundation Translation Prize.

Gary Rafferty served in the U.S. Army in Vietnam in 1970 and 1971 along the DMZ and west to the Laos border. He retired from the Nashua, New Hampshire Fire Department as a lieutenant in 1991. His first book of poetry, *Marble Soup,* is due to be released in 1998 by Whirlwind Press.

Elliot Richman published his first poem in 1984, when he was forty-two years old. In 1993 he won a Creative Writers' Fellowship from the National Endowment for the Arts, and a New York Foundation for the Arts Fellowship in Poetry. In addition to *Walk On,* published in 1994, Richman's two chapbooks centered around the Vietnam War are *A Bucket of Nails: Poems from the Second IndoChina War* and *Dispatches: From Vietnam to the Garden of Earthly Delights* (with Bill Shields), reissued by the Lunar Offensive Press in 1996.

Dale Ritterbusch served in the U.S. Army from 1966 to 1969. After receiving his commission from the Infantry School at Fort Benning, he served as a training officer and hazardous munitions escort officer before being attached to JUS-MAAG/MACTHAI, where he was responsible for coordinating shipments of aerial mines for dispersal along the Ho Chi Minh Trail. He is an associate professor in the Department of Languages and Literature at the University of Wisconsin, Whitewater.

Richard Ryan was born in Dublin, and is the author of *Ledges* and *Ravenswood.*

The late **James Schuyler** won the Pulitzer Prize for poetry in 1981. He published several books of poetry and two novels.

Tom V. Schmidt has been the poetry instructor for the Harmony Arts Mobile Unit since 1980. During the Vietnam War he served in the National Guard. His duties included unloading bodies from cargo planes in from Vietnam, and reloading them onto trucks to Oakland. He has been a jazz clarinetist for the past twenty-two years.

Dick Shea served as a lieutenant in the naval forces from 1961–65. He was one of the first SEALS to serve in Vietnam. He moved to New York City and worked for the city as a night superintendent of a women's shelter until 1994, when he retired after twenty-six years.

Bill Shields did two tours in Vietnam, 1969–70, and again in 1972. He has three books in print—*Human Shrapnel, The Southeast Asian Book of the Dead,* and *Lifetaker*—all published by 2.13.61 Publications. He currently lives in Harrisburg, Pennsylvania.

The late **A. J. M. Smith** was a Canadian poet who spent most of his life teaching at Michigan State University, where he was poet in residence during the 1960s and early 1970s. He was horrified at what the United States was doing to Vietnam and to a generation of young people.

The late **George Starbuck** published six books of poetry.

Lamont Steptoe is a poet/photographer/publisher born and raised in Pittsburgh. He is the author of eight books of poetry. The latest, published in August 1997, is *In the Kitchens of the Masters* (Iniquity Press/Vendetta Books). He served in Vietnam and suffers from posttraumatic stress disorder. He is an activist in human rights, environmental, and gay/bisexual rights issues.

R. A. Streitmatter/Tran Trong Dat was named Tran Trong Dat by a Vietnamese nurse. He was born to unknown parents in 1972 and lived in a Saigon orphanage until adopted by an American family. He currently lives and works in Boston, Massachusetts. He enjoys a wonderful relationship with his family, and continues to search for lost relatives. He can be contacted at: asianaml@tiac.net.

Chris Taniguchi was born into a career military family. His father served in Vietnam from 1968 to 1970, stationed at Tan Son Nuth Airbase.

Te Hanh: No biographical information is available.

Thai Nguyen: No biographical information is available.

Thien Ly: No biographical information is available.

Thich Nhat Hanh was chair of the Buddhist Peace Delegation to the Paris Peace Accords during the Vietnam War. He was nominated for the Nobel Peace Prize by Dr. Martin Luther King Jr. He lives in a small retreat community in France, where he teaches, writes, gardens, and works to help refugees worldwide.

Thien-bao Thuc Phi was born just a few months before, in his words, "the fall/liberation of Saigon. My father served in the armed forces, so we were allowed to flee." He grew up in Minneapolis, Minnesota, and graduated cum laude from Macalester College in St. Paul. He is currently teaching a workshop for Asian and Asian-American teens and plans to apply to graduate school.

Thuong Vuong-Riddick was born in Hanoi in 1940, during the French regime. In 1962 she traveled to Paris, where she acquired a second BA, an MA, and her doctorate. In 1969 she immigrated to Canada where she taught literature at the University of Montreal and at McGill University. In 1981 she moved to Victoria, British Columbia, where she taught at the University of Victoria.

To Huu was born in Hue, central Vietnam, in 1920. Publishing his first poems at the age of seventeen, he was imprisoned by the French authorities from 1939 to 1942, when he escaped and began active involvement as a Communist in the war of independence.

Ton That Lap is a well-known folk singer and member of the student antiwar movement in South Vietnam.

Barbara Tran is a second-generation Vietnamese American and a native New Yorker. She is the coeditor of *Watermark: Vietnamese-American Poetry & Prose,* published in 1997 by Magic 99 Press. Her own poems have appeared in *Amerasia Journal, The Viet Nam Forum, Antioch Review,* and *Ploughshares.* She is the recipient of fellowships from the Millay and MacDowell colonies.

Tran Da Tu: No biographical information is available.

Tran Duc Uyen: No biographical information is available.

Tran Mong Tu was born in Vietnam. During the war, she worked for the Associated Press in Saigon. She is a well-known poet and short story writer in the global Vietnamese community. Since arriving in the United States in 1975, she has published three works of poetry and short stories. She now lives in Washington State with her family.

Tran Thi Nga was born in North Vietnam and moved to Saigon, where she worked in the *Time* magazine office. She now lives in the United States.

Trinh Cong Son was a well-known folk singer and member of the student antiwar movement in South Vietnam.

Trinh T. Minh-Ha was born in Vietnam. A filmmaker, writer, and composer, she is currently professor of Women's Studies and Film at the University of California, Berkeley.

Truong Quoc Khanh was a member of the student antiwar movement in South Vietnam.

Truong Tran is a graduate student in creative writing at San Francisco State University. His poems have appeared in numerous literary journals. Truong says his poems explore the "cultural crossings of being Vietnamese American."

Tu-Uyen Nguyen was named after a male poet character in a Vietnamese folktale. She was born in Saigon in 1972 and immigrated to the United States with her parents and younger brother in 1979 as a "boat person." Currently, she is a graduate student in the School of Public Health at UCLA. She hopes to continue writing to document the experiences of Vietnamese-American families so that this valuable history is not lost.

Lewis Turco served in the U.S. Navy 1952–56. During 1953–54 he patrolled the straits of Formosa (now Taiwan) aboard the USS *Hornet* (CVA12) while the French were fighting in "IndoChina." One day when the Chinese fishing fleet surrounded the *Hornet* from horizon to horizon, he states he "realized the hopelessness of fighting a war in Asia. I therefore participated in the first 'Poets for Peace' reading in Cleveland in 1962." He is the founding director of both the Cleveland State University Poetry Center and the Program in Writing Arts at SUNY, Oswego, from which he retired in 1996 as professor of English and poet in residence. He is the author of numerous books of poetry.

Peter Ulisse served as first lieutenant, U.S. Army, 1968–70. Served in Vietnam in 1969 in Bien Hoa. Currently English professor and chair of the humanities department at Housatonic Community Technical College in Bridgeport, Connecticut. He has published well over a hundred poems in various journals and magazines across the country.

David Vancil was a child of a military family. With an ROTC commission, he served two years of active duty. He was promoted to first lieutenant while serving as a MACV adviser on Mobile Advisory Team II-19. He received his PhD in English from the University of Southwestern Louisiana in December 1995. He has published poetry, fiction, literary criticism, and scholarly works. His *Catalog of Dictionaries* has been called a standard work in the field of library science.

Bruce Weigl is the author of seven books of poetry. His poetry, essays, articles, and reviews have appeared widely, and he currently teaches in the writing program at Penn State University. Born in Lorain, Ohio, Weigl served in Vietnam with the First Air Cavalry, where he was awarded a Bronze Star.

David Widup served in Vietnam with the U.S. Air Force from September 1969 to September 1970. He was discharged honorably in 1972 and went on to get an MA in economics and an advanced degree in computer applications and information science from New York University. David marks the Vietnam veterans' parade in New York City in 1985 as the beginning of his writing career and his recovery from the war.

Linda Williamson: No biographical information is available.

Xuan Moi: See the note regarding *Poems from Captured Documents* under Ky Niem Thanh Dang.

ACKNOWLEDGMENTS

Doug Anderson
- "Ambush"
- "Outliving Our Ghosts"
- "Short Timer"
- "Bamboo Bridge"
- "Xin Loi"

From *The Moon Reflected Fire* by Doug Anderson. Farmington, ME: Alice James Books, 1994.

Margaret Atwood
- "It Is Dangerous to Read Newspapers"

"It Is Dangerous to Read Newspapers" from *Selected Poems 1966–1984* by Margaret Atwood. Copyright © Margaret Atwood 1990. Reprinted by permission of Oxford University Press Canada.

John Balaban
- "April 30, 1975"

From *Blue Mountain* (Greensboro, NC: Unicorn Press, 1980) by permission of the author.
- "For the Missing in Action"
- "In Celebration of Spring"

From *Locusts at the Edge of Summer,* copyright © 1997 by John Balaban. Reprinted by permission of Copper Canyon Press, P.O. Box 271, Port Townsend, WA 98368.

Bao-Long Chu
- "Mother's Pearls"

From *Once Upon a Dream: The Vietnamese-American Experience,* De Tran, Andrew Lam, and Hai Dai Nguyen, eds. Kansas City: Andrews and McMeel, 1995.
- "Letter from Bac Ninh, Written to a Brother in America"
- "This Is the House I Pass Through Daily"

Previously unpublished.

• "M.I.A."
Vietnam Forum # 16 (1997), Yale Southeast Asia Studies. New Haven, CT.

JAN BARRY
• "A Nun in Ninh Hoa"
From *Carrying the Darkness,* Ehrhart, W. D., ed. Lubbock, TX: Texas Tech University Press, 1985.
• "The Longest War"
From *Winning Hearts and Minds,* Rottman, Larry, and Jan Barry, and Basil T. Paquet, eds. Brooklyn, NY: 1ˢᵗ Casualty Press, 1972.
• "The Peace Monument"
From *Veterans Day* by Barry, Jan. Richford, VT: Samisdat, 1983.

R. L. BARTH
• "For the Memory of Thich Quang Duc"
From *Simonides in Vietnam* by R. L. Barth. Santa Barbara, Calif.: John Daniel, 1990.
• "P.O.W.'s"
• "The Insert"
From *A Soldier's Time* by R. L. Barth. Santa Barbara, CA: John Daniel, 1987.

BILL BAUER
• "A Vietnam Veteran's Memorial Day"
From *Promises in the Dust* by Bill Bauer. Kansas City: BkMk Press, 1995.

DANIEL BERRIGAN
• "Reading the Poems of Ho"
• "We Were Permitted to Meet Together in Prison to Prepare for Trial"
From *Prison Poems* by Daniel Berrigan. Greensboro, NC: Unicorn Press, 1973.

D. C. BERRY
• "Gulf of Tonkin"
The Gettysburg Review 9, no. 4 (Autumn 1996). Reprinted here with permission of the editors of *The Gettysburg Review.*

GEORGE BILGERE
• "At the Vietnam Memorial"
Poetry, June 1995, CLXVI, 3: 141. Copyright © 1995 by The Modern Poetry Association. Reprinted by permission of the Editor of *Poetry.*

ROBERT BLY
- "Counting Small-Boned Bodies"
- "At a March Against the Vietnam War"
- "Driving Through Minnesota During the Hanoi Bombings"
From *The Light Around the Body* by Robert Bly. Copyright ©1996 by Robert Bly. Reprinted by permission of HarperCollins.

KEVIN BOWEN
- "First Casualty"
- "Banded Kraits"
- "Temple at Quan Loi, 1969"
- "A Conical Hat"
From *Playing Basketball with the Viet Con* by Kevin Bowen. Willimantic, CT: Curbstone Press, 1994.

HAYDEN CARRUTH
- "On Being Asked to Write a Poem Against the War in Vietnam"
From *Collected Shorter Poems* © 1992 by Hayden Carruth
Reprinted by permission of Copper Canyon Press, P.O. Box 271, Port Townsend, WA 98368.

L. L. CASE
- "No Complaints"
Reprinted by permission of Paul Krassner and *The Realist* magazine.

FRAN CASTAN
- "Soldier's Widow: A Generic Photo"
- "Unveiling the Vietnam Memorial"
From *The Widow's Quilt* by Fran Castan. Sag Harbor, NY: Canio's Edition, 1996.

MICHAEL CASEY
- "Knowledge"
- "Prisoner of War"
- "On What the Army Does with Heads"
From *Obscenities* by Michael Casey. New Haven: Yale University Press, 1972.

HORACE COLEMAN/SHAKA AKU SHANGO
- "OK Corral East"

- "A Black Soldier Remembers:"
- "The Wall"
From *In the Grass* by Horace Coleman. Woodbridge, CT:Vietnam Generation
Inc. & Burning Cities Press, 1995.

DAVID CONNOLLY
- "Corporal Thach: First Confirmed NVA Kill"
- "It Don't Mean Nothin"
- "No Lie, GI"
- "In His Father's Footsteps"
From *Lost in America* by David Connolly. Woodbridge, CT:Vietnam Genera-
tion Inc. & Burning Cities Press, 1994.

FRANK CROSS
- "The Skull Beside a Mountain Trail"
From *Reminders* by Frank A. Cross, Jr. Big Timber, MT: Seven Buffaloes Press,
1986.

GLOVER DAVIS
- "Columns"
Poetry. CXX, 6 (1972). "Poetry Against the War" (special issue). Copyright ©
1972 by The Modern Poetry Association. Reprinted by permission of the Editor
of *Poetry.*

DO TAN
- "Words of Comfort"
(Translated by Huynh Sanh Thong)
From *An Anthology of Vietnamese Poems,* Huynh Sanh Thong, ed. New
Haven:Yale University Press, 1996.
- "Twenty Years"
(Translated by Nguyen Ngoc Bich, Burton Raffel, and W. S. Merwin)
From *A Thousand Years of Vietnamese Poetry,* Nguyen Ngoc Bich, ed. New
York:Alfred A. Knopf, 1975.

DUONG TUONG
- "At the Vietnam Wall"
Vietnam Forum 16 (1997) Yale Southeast Asia Studies. New Haven, Connecticut.

DU TU LE
- "What I Leave to My Son"

(Translated by Nguyen Ngoc Bich, Burton Raffel, and W. S. Merwin)
From *A Thousand Years of Vietnamese Poetry,* Nguyen Ngoc Bich, ed. New York: Alfred A. Knopf, 1975.

W. D. EHRHART
• "The Next Step"
• "Guerilla War"
From *Unaccustomed Mercy: Soldier Poets of the Vietnam War,* Ehrhart, W. D., ed. Lubbock, TX: Texas Tech University Press, 1989.
• "Coming Home"
"Coming Home" is reprinted from *To Those Who Have Gone Home Tired,* by W. D. Ehrhart, New York: Thunder's Mouth Press, 1984.
• "POW/MIA"
• "For Mrs. Na"
From *Just for Laughs* by W. D. Ehrhart. Silver Spring, MD: Vietnam Generation Inc. & Burning Cities Press, 1990.
• "Midnight at the Vietnam Veterans Memorial"
From *The Distance We Travel* by W. D. Ehrhart. Easthampton, MA: Adastra Press, 1993.

LIZ FARRELL
• "For Timothy Clover"
From *Peace Is Our Profession,* Barry, Jan, ed. Montclair, NJ: East River Anthology, 1981.

JAMES FENTON
• "Cambodia"
From *Children in Exile* by James Fenton. Copyright ©1985 by James Fenton. Reprinted by permission of Farrar, Straus & Giroux.

DAVID FERGUSON
• "Norman Morrison"
From *Where Is Vietnam?,* Walter Lowenfels, ed. Garden City, NY: Doubleday & Company, 1967.

BRYAN ALEC FLOYD
• "Second Lieutenant Parvin Zelmer, U.S.M.C."
• "Corporal Charles Chungtu, U.S.M.C."
From *The Long War Dead* by Bryan Alec. Floyd. Sag Harbor, NY: The Permanent Press, 1976.

SHARON FUHRMAN
• "Pete"
From *Listen. The War,* Lieutenant Colonel Fred Kiley and Lieutenant Colonel
Tony Deter, eds. United States Air Force Academy, 1973.

GIANG NAM
• "Night Crossing"
(Translated by Don Luce, John Schafer, and Jacqui Chagnon)
From *We Promise One Another: Poems from an Asian War,* Don Luce, John
C. Schafer, and Jacquelyn Chagnon, eds. Washington, DC: Indochina Mobile
Education Project, c. 1971.

ALLEN GINSBERG
• "Imaginary Universes"
From *Collected Poems 1947–1980* by Allen Ginsberg. Copyright ©1984 by
Allen Ginsberg. Reprinted by permission of HarperCollins Publishers, Inc.

JON FORREST GLADE
• "Pointman"
• "Blood Trail"
• "Viper"
• "Shitbirds"
• "Freedom Bird"
From *Photographs of the Jungle* by Jon Forrest Glade. St. John, KS: Chiron
Review Press, 1990.

EUGENE E. GROLLMES
• "At the Vietnam Veterans Memorial, Washington D.C.: Chrissie"
From *At the Vietnam Veterans Memorial, Washington D.C: Between the
Lines* by Eugene E. Grollmes. Washington, DC: Friends of the Vietnam Veterans
Memorial, 1988.

HA HUYEN CHI
• "The Sea, the World, and the Boat People"
"Songs of Exile," *Vietnam Forum* 1 (Winter–Spring 1983). Yale Southeast Asia
Studies. New Haven, CT.

J. VINCENT HANSEN
• "When"
From *Blessed Are the Piecemakers* by J. Vincent Hansen. St. Cloud, MN: North
Star Press of St. Cloud, Inc., 1989.

MICHAEL S. HARPER
• "Caves"
From *Images of Kin: New & Selected Poems* by Michael S. Harper. Urbana: University of Illinois Press, 1970.

PAULINE HEBERT
• "Luck"
Previously unpublished.

L. RUSSELL HERMAN JR.
• "Fifteenth Day of the Fourth Month of the Year 1972"
From *Peace Is Our Profession*, Barry, Jan, ed. Montclair, NJ: East River Anthology, 1981.

HHT
• "The Sea and the Sands"
(Translated by Huynh Sanh Thong)
From *An Anthology of Vietnamese Poems*, Huynh Sanh Thong, ed. New Haven: Yale University Press, 1996.

GEORGE HITCHCOCK
• "Scattering Flowers"
From *A Poetry Reading Against the Vietnam War*, Robert Bly and David Ray, eds. Madison, MN: The Sixties Press, 1966.

HOANG LIEN
• "Sitting Still"
(Translated by Huynh Sanh Thong)
Sitting Still by Hoang Lien. San Diego: The Society for Vietnamese Traditions, 1991.

HO CHI MINH
• "Pastoral Scene"
• "On the Way to Nanning"
(Translated by Don Luce, John Schafer, and Jacqui Chagnon)
From *We Promise One Another: Poems from an Asian War*, Don Luce, John C. Schafer, and Jacquelyn Chagnon, eds. Washington, DC: Indochina Mobile Education Project, c. 1971.
• "Tung Chun Prison"
(Translated by Burton Raffel)

Ho Chi Minh. "Eleven Poems by Ho Chi Minh." *TriQuarterly* 31 (Fall 1974)
Special issue: Contemporary Asian Literature.

DANIEL HOFFMAN
• "A Special Train"
From *Hang-Gliding from Helicon: New & Selected Poems* by Daniel Hoffman.
Baton Rouge: Louisiana State University Press, 1988. Reprinted here by permission of Louisiana State University Press. Copyright ©1988 by Daniel Hoffman.

DAVID HUDDLE
• "Entry"
• "Work"
• "Haircut"
• "Words"
From *Stopping by Home* by David Huddle. Salt Lake City: Peregrine Smith
Books, 1988.

RICHARD HUGO
• "On Hearing a New Escalation"
"On Hearing a New Escalation," copyright ©1972 by Richard Hugo, from *Making It Certain It Goes On: The Collected Poems of Richard Hugo.* Reprinted
by permission of W.W. Norton & Company, Inc.

LOWELL JAEGER
• "The Trial"
From *War on War* by Lowell Jaeger. Logan: Utah State University Press, 1988.

BILL JONES
• "Near Laos"
• "The Body Burning Detail"
From *Blood Trails* by Bill Jones and Rod McQueary. Lemon Cove, CA: Dry
Crik Press, 1993.

MILTON KAPLAN
• "Ballet"
From *70 on the 70's,* Robert McGowan and Richard Snyder, eds. Ashland, OH:
Ashland Poetry Press, 1981.

MARK KESSINGER
• "Dead"

• "Kids"
From *The Book of Joe* by Mark Kessinger. Cleveland: Cleveland State University
Poetry Center, 1990. Copyright ©1990 by Mark Kessinger.

DENIS KNIGHT
• "Schoolday in Man Quang"
From *Where Is Vietnam?* Walter Lowenfels, ed. Garden City, NY: Doubleday,
1967.

YUSEF KOMUNYAKAA
• "We Never Know"
• "Tunnels"
• " 'You and I Are Disappearing' "
• "Report from the Skull's Diorama"
• "*Dui Boi,* Dust of Life"
From *Dien Cai Dau,* copyright © 1988 by Yusef Komunyakaa, Wesleyan Univer-
sity Press, by permission of University Press of New England.

HERBERT KROHN
• "Ballade of the Saigon Streets"
From *Winning Hearts and Minds,* Larry Rottman, Jan Barry, and Basil T.
Paquet, eds. Brooklyn, NY: 1ˢᵗ Casualty Press, 1972.

GREG KUZMA
• "Peace, So That"
Poetry. CXX, 6 (1972). "Poetry Against the War" (special issue). Copyright ©
1972 by The Modern Poetry Association. Reprinted by permission of the Editor
of *Poetry.*

KY NIEM THANH DANG
• "A Young Man's Recollection"
(Translated by Thanh T. Nguyen and Bruce Weigl)
Reprinted from *Poems From Captured Documents,* selected and translated from
the Vietnamese by Thanh T. Nguyen and Bruce Weigl. Amherst: University of
Massachusetts Press, 1994. Copyright ©© 1994 by the University of Massachu-
setts Press.

CHRISTIAN NGUYEN LANGWORTHY
• "Cicada Song"
• "Even as I Lie Pretending Sleep"

• "Sons Without Fathers"
From *The Geography of War* by Christian Nguyen Langworthy. Oklahoma
City: Cooper House Publishing Inc., 1995.
• "How I Could Interpret the Events of My Youth, Events I Do Not Remember
Except in Dreams"
From *Premonitions,* Walter K. Lew, ed. New York: Kaya Productions, 1995.

WENDY WILDER LARSEN
• "Orphanage"
From *Shallow Graves* by Wendy Wilder Larsen and Tran Thi Nga. New York:
Random House, 1986.

ROBERT LAX
• "Untitled"
From *The 1968 Peace Calendar: Out of the War Shadow,* Denise Levertov, ed.
New York: War Resisters League, 1967.

MCAVOY LAYNE
• "On the Yellow Footprints"
From *How Audie Murphy Died in Vietnam* by McAvoy Layne. Garden City,
NY: Anchor Books, 1973.

LE DAN
• "Child of My Lai"
(Translated by Don Luce, John Schafer, and Jacqui Chagnon)
From *Of Quiet Courage: Poems from Viet Nam,* Jacqui Chagnon and Don
Luce, eds. Washington, DC: Indochina Mobile Education Project, 1974.

SHARON LEE
• "Letter from Nam"
From *Peace Is Our Profession,* Jan Barry, ed. Montclair, NJ: East River Anthol-
ogy, 1981.

LE MINH THU
• "Thirteen"
(Translated by Don Luce, John Schafer, and Jacqui Chagnon)
From *Of Quiet Courage: Poems from Viet Nam,* Jacqui Chagnon and Don
Luce, eds. Washington, DC: Indochina Mobile Education Project, 1974.

LE THI MAY
• "Wind and Widow"

(Translated by Nguyen Ba Chung)
Manoa: A Pacific Journal of International Writing 7, no. 2 (1995). "Contemporary Vietnamese Literature" (special issue).

LE THI DIEM THUY
• "Shrapnel Shards on Blue Water"
Vietnam Forum 16 (1997). Yale Southeast Asia Studies, New Haven, CT.

DENISE LEVERTOV
• "The Distance"
First printed in *Poetry* CXX, 6 (1972). "Poetry Against the War" (special issue).
From *The Freeing of the Dust,* copyright ©1975 by Denise Levertov. Reprinted by permission of New Directions Publishing Corp.

PHILIP LEVINE
• "This War"
Poetry CXX, 6 (1972). "Poetry Against the War" (special issue). Copyright © 1972 by The Modern Poetry Association. Reprinted by permission of the Editor of *Poetry.*

JACK LINDEMAN
• "Uncle Sam at the Pentagon"
Chelsea 26 (1969).

JACQUELINE M. LORING
• "Curse the Rainbow"
Previously unpublished.

DON LUCE
• "America: December 1972"
From *Peace Is Our Profession,* Jan Barry, ed. Montclair, NJ: East River Anthology, 1981.
• "Christmas Eve 1972"
From *Shadows from a Cabin Night* by Don Luce. New York: The Asian Center, 1979.

LUU TRONG LU
• "Women of the South"
(Translated by Don Luce, John Schafer, and Jacqui Chagnon)
From *We Promise One Another: Poems from an Asian War,* Don Luce, John

C. Schafer, and Jacquelyn Chagnon. Washington, DC: Indochina Mobile Education Project, c. 1971.

CLARENCE MAJOR
• "Vietnam # 4
From *Where is Vietnam?,* Walter Lowenfels, ed. Garden City, NY: Doubleday, 1967. Copyright ©1967 by Clarence Major.
•"Waiter in a California Vietnam Restaurant"
Previously unpublished. Copyright ©1988 by Clarence Major.

PAUL MARTIN
• "Watching the News"
From*Carrying the Darkness,* W. D. Ehrhart, ed. Lubbock, TX: Texas Tech University Press, 1985.

HERBERT WOODWARD MARTIN
• "A Negro Soldier's Viet Nam Diary"
From *Peace Is Our Profession,* Jan Barry, ed. Montclair, NJ: East River Anthology, 1981.

STEVE MASON
• From *Closure: A Much Needed War*
From *Johnny's Song* by Steve. Mason. New York: Bantam Books, 1986.

GERALD MCCARTHY
• "Untitled" ("We found him")
• "War Story"
• "The Fall of Da Nang"
From *War Story* by Gerald McCarthy. Trumansburg, NY: Crossing Press, 1977.
• "At the Crossroads"
From *Shoetown* by Gerald McCarthy. Bristol, IN: Cloverdale Library, 1992.

NORMAN A. MCDANIEL
• "My Plight (Sonnet: 1971–1972)"
From *Yet Another Voice* by Norman A. McDaniel. New York: Hawthorn Books, 1975.

WALTER MCDONALD
• "Flight Orders"

• "Embarkation"
From *Caliban in Blue* by Walter McDonald. Lubbock: Texas Tech University Press, 1976. Reprinted with permission of the author and the publisher.
• "New Guy"
From *After the Noise of Saigon* by Walter McDonald. Amherst: University of Massachusetts Press, 1988.
• "Taking Aim"
From *Burning the Fence* by Walter McDonald. Lubbock: Texas Tech University Press, copyright ©1981. Reprinted with permission of the author and the publisher.
• "After the Fall of Saigon"
From *Counting Survivors* by Walter McDonald. Copyright ©1995. Reprinted by permission of the University of Pittsburgh Press.

ROD MCQUEARY
• "White Wall"
From *Blood Trails by* Bill Jones and Rod McQueary. Lemon Cove, CA: Dry Crik Press, 1993.

W. S. MERWIN
• "The Asians Dying"
From *Naked Poetry: Recent American Poetry in Open Forms,* Stephen Berg and Robert Mezey, eds. New York: Bobbs-Merrill Company, 1969.

JEFF MILLER
• "Where Does It End?"
From *Peace Is Our Profession,* Jan Barry ed. Montclair, NJ: East River Anthology, 1981.

MINH DUNG
• "A Mother's Evening Meditation"
(Translated by Nguyen Ngoc Bich, Burton Raffel, and W. S. Merwin)
From *A Thousand Years of Vietnamese Poetry,* Nguyen Ngoc Bich, ed. New York: Alfred A. Knopf, 1975.

MINH VIEN
• "Saigon: The Unhealed Wound"
From *Saigon, The Unhealed Wound* by Minh Vien. San Francisco: Moonlit Garden, 1990.

L. Dean Minze
• "Mission"
From *Listen. The War,* Lieutenant Colonel Fred Kiley and Lieutenant Colonel Tony Deter, eds. United States Air Force Academy, 1973.

Mong Lan
• "Three-Letter Word"
• "Tombstones"
Previously unpublished.

Ngo Vinh Long
• "Untitled" ("On this land")
From *Peace Is Our Profession,* Jan Barry, ed. Montclair, NJ: East River Anthology, 1981.

Nguyen Chi Thien
• "Do You Know That, Inside the Cruel Jail"
• "As Those Americans Flee"
(Translated by Huynh Sanh Thong)
From *Flowers From Hell* by Nguyen Chi Thien. New Haven, CT: Yale Southeast Asia Studies: 1984.

Nguyen Dinh Thi
• "Yearning"
(Translated by Huynh Sanh Thong)
From *An Anthology of Vietnamese Poems,* Huynh Sanh Thong, ed. New Haven, CT: Yale University Press, 1996.

Nguyen Ngoc Phuong
• "My Blood, My Bones"
(Translated by Don Luce, John Schafer, and Jacqui Chagnon)
From *Of Quiet Courage: Poems from Viet Nam,* Jacqui Chagnon and Don Luce, eds. Washington, DC: Indochina Mobile Education Project, 1974.

Nguyen Quang Thieu
• "On the Highway"
• "Nightmare"
• "A Song of My Native Village"
(Translated by the author and Martha Collins)
From *The Woman Carry River Water* by Nguyen Quang Thieu, edited and

translated by Martha Collins and Nguyen Quang Thieu. Amherst: University of Massachusetts Press, 1997.

NGUYEN QUOC VINH
• "Elegy to an Unwept Soldier"
Nguyen Quoc Vinh. "Elegy to an Unwept Soldier." *Vietnam Forum* 14 (1994). Yale Southeast Asia Studies, New Haven CT.

LIEUTENANT NGUYEN VAN NGHIA
• "I Stand Here"
• "From My Heart of Hearts"
(Translated by Rick Murphy and Nguyen Dinh Thich)
From *Kontum Diary* by Paul Reed and Ted Schwarz. Arlington, TX: The Summit Publishing Group, 1996.

NHAT CHI MAI
• "I Kneel Down and Pray"
(Translated by Don Luce, John Schafer, and Jacqui Chagnon)
From *Of Quiet Courage: Poems from Viet Nam,* Jacqui Chagnon and Don Luce, eds. Washington, DC: Indochina Mobile Education Project, 1974.

NHAT HANH
• "Lament of Ben Hai River"
(Translated by the author and Helen Coutant)
From *Vietnam Poems* by Nhat Hanh. Santa Barbara, CA: Unicorn Press, 1972.

JIM NYE
• "First One"
• "No Slack"
• "It's Too Late"
From *Aftershock, Poems and Prose of the Vietnam War* by Jim Nye. El Paso, TX: Cinco Puntos Press, 1991.

SHARON OLDS
• "May 1968"
From *The Wellspring* by Sharon Olds. New York: Alfred A. Knopf, 1996

GRACE PALEY
• "Two Villages"

From *Visions of War, Dreams of Peace,* Lynda Van Devanter and Joan A. Furey, eds. New York: Warner Books, 1991.

PHAM TIEN DUAT
• "The Moon in Circles of Flame"
(Translated by Nguyen Quang Thieu and Kevin Bowen)
• "In the Labor Market at Giang Vo"
(Translated by Nguyen Ba Chung and Kevin Bowen)
From *Manoa: A Pacific Journal of International Writing* 7,.no. 2 (1995). "Contemporary Vietnamese Literature" (special issue).

LEROY V. QUINTANA
• "Jump School—First Day"
• "First Encounter"
• "The First"
• "The Last Detail"
From *Interrogations* by Leroy V. Quintana. Chevy Chase, MD: Vietnam Generation Inc. & Burning Cities Press, 1990.

GARY RAFFERTY
• "Last Asylum"
• "Twins"
Previously unpublished.

ELLIOT RICHMAN
• "The Woman He Killed"
• "The Labyrinth"
• "A Poison Tree"
From *Walk on Trooper* by Elliot Richman. Woodbridge, CT: Vietnam Generation Inc. & Burning Cities Press, 1994.

DALE RITTERBUSCH
• "Humpin' Through the Boonies"
• "Intelligence"
• "Search and Destroy"
• "Interrogation"
From *Lessons Learned* by Dale Ritterbursch. Woodbridge, CT: Vietnam Generation Inc. & Burning Cities Press, 1995.

RICHARD RYAN
• "From My Lai the Thunder Went West"

From *Contemporary Irish Poetry,* Anthony Bradley, ed. Berkeley: University of California Press, 1980.

JAMES SCHUYLER
• "May, 1972"
First printed in *Poetry* CXX, 6 (1972). "Poetry Against the War" (special issue).From *Collected Poems* by James Schuyler. Copyright ©1993 by the Estate of James Schuyler. Reprinted by permission of Farrar, Straus & Giroux, Inc.

TOM V. SCHMIDT
• "Butter"
From *New American and Canadian Poetry,* John Gill, ed. Boston: Beacon Press, 1971.

DICK SHEA
• Untitled ("so for some unknown reason")
• Untitled ("marine sitting in the position")
• Untitled ("went to a barber shop today")
• Untitled ("I feel nothing")
From *Vietnam Simply* by Dick Shea. Coronado, CA: The Pro Tem Publishers, 1967.

BILL SHIELDS
• "The Sadness"
• "Peer group"
• "Nam Nightmares"
• "Tracks of My Tears"
From *Human Shrapnel* by Bill Shield. Los Angeles, CA: 2.13.61 Publications, 1991.
• "Miles of Bones"
Vietnam Generation 3N 3 (November 1991).

A. J. M. SMITH
• "Lines Written on the Occasion of President Nixon's Address to the Nation, May 8, 1972"
Poetry. CXX, 6 (1972). "Poetry Against the War" (special issue). Copyright © 1972 by The Modern Poetry Association. Reprinted by permission of the Editor of *Poetry.*

GEORGE STARBUCK
• "Of Late"

From *The Argot Merchant Disaster* by George Starbuck. Boston: Little, Brown, and Company, 1982. Copyright © 1966 by George Starbuck; first appeared in *Poetry*. By permission of Little, Brown and Company.

LAMONT STEPTOE
- "Before Going"
- "Ambush"
- "Deep as the Sea"
- "Returning the Missing"
From *Mad Minute* by Lamont Steptoe. Camden, NJ: Whirlwind Press, 1990.

R. A. STREITMATTER/TRAN TRONG DAT
- "Bui Doi 2"
- "Bui Doi 7"
- "Bui Doi"
Previously unpublished.

CHRIS TANIGUCHI
- "In Southeast Asia"
From *Manoa: A Pacific Journal of International Writing* 7, no. 2 (1995). "Contemporary Vietnamese Literature" (special issue).

TE HANH
- "Home"
(Translated by Nguyen Ngoc Bich.)
Hudson Review XX, 3 (1967): 361–68.

THAI NGUYEN
- "Let Us Stand Up"
(Translated by Don Luce, John Schafer, and Jacqui Chagnon)
Luce, Don, John C. Schafer, and Jacquelyn Chagnon. *We Promise One Another: Poems from an Asian War*. Washington, D.C.: Indochina Mobile Education Project, c. 1971.

THICH NHAT HANH
- "Condemnation"
- "Peace"
- "I Met You in the Orphanage Yard"
- "The Boat People"

Reprinted from *Call Me by My True Names: The Collected Poems of Thich Nhat Hahn* (1993) by Thich Nhat Hanh, with permission of the Parallax Press, Berkeley, California.

THIEN LY
• "Poem of Hope"
(Translated by Don Luce, John Schafer, and Jacqui Chagnon)
From *We Promise One Another: Poems from an Asian War*, Don Luce, John C. Schafer, and Jacquelyn Chagnon, eds. Washington, DC: Indochina Mobile Education Project, c. 1971.

THIEN-BAO THUC PHI
• "Home"
• "Waiting for a Cyclo in the Hood"
Previously unpublished.

THUONG VUONG-RIDDICK
• "My Beloved Is Dead in Vietnam"
• "History"
• "Blues"
From *Two Shores: Deux Rives* by Thuong Vuong-Riddick. Vancouver: Ronsdale Press, 1995.

TO HUU
• "Luom"
(Translated by Keith Bosley)
From *The War Wife: Vietnamese Poetry*, Keith Bosley, ed. London: Allison & Busby Limited, 1972.

TON THAT LAP
• "Song from Prison"
(Translated by Don Luce, John Schafer, and Jacqui Chagnon)
From *Of Quiet Courage: Poems from Viet Nam*, Jacqui Chagnon and Don Luce, eds. Washington, DC: Indochina Mobile Education Project, 1974.

BARBARA TRAN
• "The Women Next Door"
From *The Seamstress Cycle and Other Poems* by Barbara Tran. Copyright ©1996 by Barbara Tran.

TRAN DA TU
- "Gifts as Tokens of Love"
- "A Drinking Song"
- "The New Lullaby"
(Translated by Huynh Sanh Thong)
From *An Anthology of Vietnamese Poems,* Huynh Sanh Thong, ed. and trans. New Haven: Yale University Press, 1996.

TRAN DUC UYEN
- "A Letter to My father Child"
(Translated by Huynh Sanh Thong)
From *An Anthology of Vietnamese Poems,* Huynh Sanh Thong, ed. New Haven: Yale University Press, 1996.

TRAN MONG TU
- "A New Year's Wish for a Little Refugee"
(Translated by "Songs of Exile." *Vietnam Forum* 1 (Winter–Spring 1983): 106–16.

TRAN THI NGA
- "Packing"
- "The Airport"
- "Escape"
- "Tet in America"
From *Shallow Graves* by Wendy Wilder Larsen and Tran Thi Nga. New York: Random House, 1986.

TRINH CONG SON
- "Love Song of a Woman Maddened by the War"
(Translated by Don Luce, John Schafer, and Jacqui Chagnon)
From *We Promise One Another: Poems from an Asian War,* Don Luce, John C. Schafer, and Jacquelyn Chagnon, eds. Washington, DC: Indochina Mobile Education Project, c. 1971.

TRINH T. MINH-HA
- "For Love of Another"
Originally published in French as "Par amour pour autrui" in Trinh T. Minh-Ha. *En minuscule.* Paris: Le Meridien, 1987.
- "Flying Blind"

• "Refugee"
City Lights Review 4 (1990).

TRUONG QUOC KHANH
• "Devotion"
(Translated by Don Luce, John Schafer, and Jacqui Chagnon)
From *Of Quiet Courage: Poems from Viet Nam,* Jacqui Chagnon and Don
Luce, eds. Washington, DC: Indochina Mobile Education Project, 1974.

TRUONG TRAN
• "Scars"
North Dakota Quarterly 61, 3 (Summer 1993).
• "Between Thumb and Index Finger"
Prairie Schooner (Winter 1995).

TU-UYEN NGUYEN
• "Umbilical Cord"
Previously unpublished.

LEWIS TURCO
• "Burning the News"
From *The Shifting Web: New & Selected Poems* by Lewis Turco. Fayetteville:
University of Arkansas Press, 1989.

PETER ULISSE
• "Doctor Able"
• "Captain Mainero"
From *Vietnam Voices* by Peter Ulisse. Lewiston, NY: The Edward Mellen Press,
1990.

UNKNOWN
• "Postscript After Xuan Dieu"
(Translated by Keith Bosley)
From *The War Wife: Vietnamese Poetry,* Bosley, Keith, ed. London: Allison &
Busby Limited, 1972.
• "Meeting"
(Translated by Thanh T. Nguyen and Bruce Weigl)
From *Poems from Captured Documents,* Thanh T. Nguyen and Bruce Weigl,